DEVIL'S ADVOCATES

DEVIL'S ADVOCATES is a series of books devoted to exploring the classics of horror cinema. Contributors to the series come from the fields of teaching, academia, journalism and fiction, but all have one thing in common: a passion for the horror film and a desire to share it with the widest possible audience.

'The admirable Devil's Advocates series is not only essential – and fun – reading for the serious horror fan but should be set texts on any genre course.'
Dr Ian Hunter, Reader in Film Studies, De Montfort University, Leicester

'Auteur Publishing's new Devil's Advocates critiques on individual titles... offer bracingly fresh perspectives from passionate writers. The series will perfectly complement the BFI archive volumes.' **Christopher Fowler,** *Independent on Sunday*

'Devil's Advocates has proven itself more than capable of producing impassioned, intelligent analyses of genre cinema... quickly becoming the go-to guys for intelligent, easily digestible film criticism.' ***HorrorTalk.com***

'Auteur Publishing continue the good work of giving serious critical attention to significant horror films.' ***Black Static***

facebook DevilsAdvocatesbooks

DevilsAdBooks

ALSO AVAILABLE IN THIS SERIES

A Girl Walks Home Alone at Night Farshid Kazemi

Black Sunday Martyn Conterio

The Blair Witch Project Peter Turner

Blood and Black Lace Roberto Curti

The Blood on Satan's Claw David Evans-Powell

Candyman Jon Towlson

Cannibal Holocaust Calum Waddell

Carrie Neil Mitchell

The Company of Wolves James Gracey

Creepshow Simon Brown

Cruising Eugenio Ercolani & Marcus Stiglegger

The Curse of Frankenstein Marcus K. Harmes

Daughters of Darkness Kat Ellinger

Dead of Night Jez Conolly & David Bates

The Descent James Marriot

The Devils Darren Arnold

Don't Look Now Jessica Gildersleeve

The Fly Emma Westwood

Frenzy Ian Cooper

Halloween Murray Leeder

House of Usher Evert Jan van Leeuwen

In the Mouth of Madness Michael Blyth

It Follows Joshua Grimm

Ju-on The Grudge Marisa Hayes

Let the Right One In Anne Billson

M Samm Deighan

Macbeth Rebekah Owens

The Mummy Doris V. Sutherland

Nosferatu Cristina Massaccesi

Peeping Tom Kiri Bloom Walden

Saw Benjamin Poole

Scream Steven West

The Shining Laura Mee

Shivers Luke Aspell

The Silence of the Lambs Barry Forshaw

Suspiria Alexandra Heller-Nicholas

The Texas Chain Saw Massacre James Rose

The Thing Jez Conolly

Trouble Every Day Kate Robertson

Twin Peaks: Fire Walk With Me Lindsay Hallam

Witchfinder General Ian Cooper

FORTHCOMING

[REC] Jim Harper

The Evil Dead Lloyd Haynes

Repulsion Jeremy Carr

Devil's Advocates

The Conjuring

Kevin J. Wetmore, Jr.

Acknowledgements

Thanks to John Atkinson of Auteur/LUP, and to Nikki Hamlett and Charlie Brigden.

Thanks to my family – Kevin I, Eleanor, Lisa, John, Sean, Tom, Eileen, Toni, and Kevin III, Cordelia, and especially Lacy, forever the Lorraine to my Ed.

Thanks to Ian McDonald and Julia Gelb-Zimmerman for the friendship and conversations.

Lorraine Warren passed away while I wrote this book. May she rest in peace.

This book is dedicated to Tom, Mary Ann, Shae and Kaleigh Quinn – may there be no demons in your corner of Rhode Island.

First published in 2021 by
Auteur, an imprint of
Liverpool University Press,
4 Cambridge Street,
Liverpool
L69 7ZU

Series design: Nikki Hamlett at Cassels Design
Set by Cassels Design

All stills from *The Conjuring* are © New Line Cinema / The Safran Company / Evergreen Media Group.

All rights reserved. No part of this publication may be reproduced in any material form (including photocopying or storing in any medium by electronic means and whether or not transiently or incidentally to some other use of this publication) without the permission of the copyright owner.

British Library Cataloguing-in-Publication Data
A catalogue record for this book is available from the British Library

ISBN paperback: 978-1-80085-927-2
ISBN hardback: 978-1-80085-926-5
ISBN epub: 978-1-80085-808-4
ISBN PDF: 978-1-80034-397-9

Contents

Introduction: Seeing Demons 7

Chapter One: "It's right behind you!" or Rated R for "Terror" 15

Chapter Two: The Warren Files, or "Based on a true story" 39

Chapter Three: Child's Play and Women's Work 65

Chapter Four: "Everything you see in here is either haunted, cursed, or has been
  used in some kind of ritualistic practice." Or, The Endless *Conjuring* Universe 79

Conclusion: What Exactly is Conjured in *The Conjuring*? 103

Notes 107

Bibliography 109

Introduction: Seeing Demons

> All the fathers of the church, without exception, believed in the power of magic. The
> church always condemned magic, but always believed in it. It did not excommunicate
> sorcerers as deluded fools, but as men who really had dealings with devils.
> Voltaire, *Philosophical Dictionary* (1764)

True story – in the winter of 1996 I had lunch with Ed and Lorraine Warren at their house, toured their occult museum, and saw the actual Annabelle with my own eyes. When Ed was still alive, one could pay for a private session with them at their home to learn about the paranormal. Tom, my best friend, and I wanted to spend time with this couple, about whom we had read and been fascinated by for years growing up in Connecticut, just a few towns over from where the Warrens lived. We had seen the films based on their cases, read the books about them, and learned through an associate how to reach out to them, and so we arranged for an afternoon with the Warrens.

Snow was still on the ground in Monroe, the sky was overcast. We parked on the shoveled driveway and knocked on the door. It opened and Lorraine Warren herself welcomed us in. There she was – the woman we had seen on so many television specials about hauntings and ghost hunting, standing in the doorway of her own home in a bathrobe, hair wrapped in a towel, shaking our hands and encouraging us to remove coats and come in. She told us not to mind her; she just got out of the shower and Ed was waiting for us "in there," gesturing towards an archway, through which we moved.

Ed sat in an easy chair in the living room.

> "Boys," he said by means of greeting and pointed towards the sofa perpendicular to his chair. We sat.
>
> "Have you seen a demon, boys?" he began, continuing without waiting for an answer from us. "I've seen demons." He made eye contact with me as if to ensure I understood. "You wouldn't want to see a demon."

Ed told us stories for hours. He told us of Maurice the werewolf, the Amityville case, Annabelle the cursed doll, poltergeists and demons (it always came back to demons), the Smurl case, and so many others. When we told him we were from Cheshire, a nearby Connecticut town, he told us about the Snedeker case from Southington, the town next to ours, later dramatized in *A Haunting in Connecticut* (2009, Peter Cornwell). Lorraine made bologna sandwiches, which we ate in the living room while Ed continued to tell us of cases in between bites of bologna.

"You boys ready?" he asked at last.

"Yes, sir," we replied.

"Touch nothing. Don't mock or make fun of anything. Take this seriously, because there are objects in there that can kill you."

Lorraine then escorted us to their museum of occult and paranormal artefacts.

"Aren't you coming in with us?" I asked.

"Oh, no, dear. You boys will be fine. Just follow the rules and you'll learn a great deal about how we are constantly at war with the forces of darkness."

We entered, and there she was, in a glass case at eye level: Annabelle, whom, unlike in the films, is actually an old Raggedy Ann doll.[1] She was purchased in a thrift store by a woman who gifted it to her daughter, a nurse. The doll would allegedly write and leave notes while the nurse was at work and be found in places other than where it was left, and allegedly attacked a man, leaving claw marks. We saw a number of purportedly cursed and haunted objects. I must be honest: the room was very, very cold. It was winter in New England, and there did not appear to be any sources of heat in the space. And Ed had certainly prepped us with two hours of stories of the supernatural, but I still remember the room being unusually cold, even for that time of year.

I thought of that visit to the Warrens again when I first saw *The Conjuring* (2013, James Wan) upon its initial release almost twenty years after our visit to their home. Annabelle was different, the occult artefact room in the film looked very different from the real one, and Ed had never told us about the Perrons. But when I watched the film, I was back in that house in Monroe, in one of the coldest spaces I have encountered, facing objects supposedly haunted or possessed, remembering Ed's warning – that I should not want to see a demon. Yet to be a horror fan is to want to see demons. *The Conjuring* Universe, as it is called, brings one face to face with them repeatedly.

Directed by James Wan, who had previously helmed *Insidious* (2010), another popular ghost story that turned out to be more than a ghost story, *The Conjuring* opened on 19 July 2013, an unusual time to release a horror film, and yet economically it made sense to do so. The film had originally been scheduled for a spring release, but remarkably positive responses from test audiences convinced Warner Brothers and New Line Cinema to release it during the summer blockbuster season. Based on box office and critical reception, they were right to do so.

The film was a critical and popular success. It earned an impressive $41.5 million on its opening weekend, which made it the best-debut for an R-rated horror film to date. *The New York Times* review called it "a fantastically effective haunted-house movie" and "the next great shocker" (Dargis 2013). *Variety* called it Wan's best film to date, noting his "command of horror technique isn't just virtuosic; it's borderline rhapsodic, playing the audience like Hitchcock's proverbial piano" (Chang 2013, 88). *The A.V. Club* review called it "an exercise in classical scare tactics, delivered through an escalating series of primo setpieces…often supremely effective" (Dowd 2013). Writing for *Screenrant*, Kofi Outlaw calls it "a very satisfying horror movie" and "the scariest movie of 2013 (so far)" (Outlaw 2013). Reviews upon release and subsequent to it have been glowing, praising the film as genuinely terrifying and well made, with almost all of them citing Wan's work as masterful.

Not everyone was a fan. The critic for the *Austin Chronicle* condescended, "It might as well be retitled 'The Amityville Exorcist'," claiming that it was an example of "blatant thievery" from older films, and in the end was "ear-splitting nonsense" (Davis 2013). Although Kofi Outlaw praises the film, he also notes, "when it's done – beyond the trauma of a freaky moviegoing experience – there is little to ponder or reflect upon" (Outlaw 2013). Such critiques, however, were in the minority. While some critics found it derivative of older horror movies, many critics viewed the film as an example *par excellence* of the genre, rather than a copycat of it, with *The Wrap* critic Alonso Duralde effectively arguing, "Fred Astaire didn't invent tap-dancing," he just did it better than anyone else (Duralde 2013).

I find *The Conjuring* to be "culturally intertextual," to employ Douglas E. Cowan's term, as well as double coded (2008, 11). The former refers to the idea that much of the content is culturally referential and makes more sense if one is aware of ghost hunting shows, *The Exorcist* (1973, William Friedkin), other haunted house and possession films, and even the Warrens themselves. The latter refers to the idea that various lines and moments in the film carry more resonance if one is "on the inside." The filmmakers have stated their intention in making a Christian, and specifically a Catholic horror film. If one is Catholic or knows Catholicism, certain lines mean differently than their surface meaning. Lastly, the combination of the two ideas means the film is not just self-referential, but highly referential to both the world of horror and the world of the Warrens. For example, at the end of the film Lorraine tells Ed that their priest wants to speak to them about "a case in Long Island." Nothing more is said, but the canny viewer knows this is a reference to the Amityville haunting, in which the Lutz family claimed that their home in Amityville, Long Island, was haunted, as detailed in the book and film *The Amityville Horror* (1979, Stuart Rosenberg). The film never mentions the word "Amityville," so this is an example of needing the referential knowledge to understand the larger meaning of the film.

Similarly, the more one is familiar with the horror genre, the more Wan's film reads as a masterclass in creating and sustaining tension based on models from the seventies through the twenty-first century. *The Conjuring* is a blend of the slow horror of *Paranormal Activity* (2007, Oren Pelli) and *The Babadook* (2014, Jennifer Kent) with more traditional horror elements into an amalgam of horror sub-genres: haunted house, possession, slasher, and found footage. The Perron house hides demons, the ghost of a witch, the spirit of a dead boy killed at the witch's behest, and other spectres. The film is also the height (so far) of Wan's work as a horror director, surpassing *Saw* (2004) and *Insidious* in terms of how it creates its scares.

The film has proven to have a successful legacy as well. By 2017, with the release of *Annabelle: Creation* (dir. David F. Sandberg), the fourth film in the franchise, the *Conjuring* films surpassed a billion dollars at the global box office. A press release from New Line Cinema, co-distributor of the film, crowed, "James Wan has a proven ability to tap into minds of horror fans in a way few can. To reach this benchmark with just four films is truly remarkable" (New Line Cinema 2017). Those numbers have only grown with the next three films, although, as will be explored in chapter four, the law of diminishing returns means the most recent *Conjuring* Universe films, *The Curse of La Llorona* (2019,

Michael Chaves) and *Annabelle Comes Home* (2019, Gary Dauberman) are perceived by critics as being lesser lights in the series, derivative and missing what made *The Conjuring* original and unique.

This volume explores *The Conjuring* and its offspring in four chapters. *The Conjuring* was rated R for "terror" by the Motion Picture Association of America. In chapter one, "'It's right behind you!' or Rated R for 'Terror,'" we examine that ratings classification, why it is merited, and the three most frightening moments in the film as exemplars of how James Wan manipulates the audience and develops slow scares. It then contextualizes *The Conjuring* with Wan's previous work and considers his collaborators. After a brief production history, the chapter considers the use of humor to offset and thus heighten the horror. Lastly, the first chapter considers the importance of seeing in the film – film is a visual medium and *The Conjuring* plays around with the idea of what you can and cannot see and which is scarier.

The second chapter, "The Warren Files, or 'Based on a true story'" considers how the film was marketed as being based in reality and rooted in the Warrens' identity as the nation's preeminent paranormal investigators. The chapter compares Ed and Lorraine Warren with their fictional counterparts. It then argues that *The Conjuring* also maintains its veneer of "reality" by employing techniques from and references to paranormal investigations on television and film, wearing its religion on its sleeve while obscuring the genuine religious inaccuracies within the film, and using the bad witch trope despite all historic evidence against it. *The Conjuring* does not so much use and present reality as employ popular culture's versions of reality (and ghosts, religion and witches) in order to craft a horrific, scary narrative.

The third chapter, "Child's Play and Women's Work" examines children and women in the film. In particular, *The Conjuring* is a film filled with dangerous and diabolical toys and games: the doll Annabelle, the game Hide-and-Clap, Rory's music box, the haunted toys in the Warrens' Occult Museum. The film also depicts children in peril and the parents who must struggle to protect them, even as the danger often comes (directly or indirectly) from the parents themselves. The five Perron daughters are linked with Judy Warren, Ed and Lorraine's daughter, as all are threatened by supernatural evil and the threat of being harmed by the parents. In contrast, the film also shows Rory, the dead boy killed by his mother, as a cautionary tale. Similarly, *The Conjuring* is a female-centric movie, concerned with wives and mothers, and yet is not particularly feminist. The second half of chapter three offers a feminist reading of the women of *The Conjuring*.

Lastly, in chapter four, entitled "'Everything you see in here is either haunted, cursed, or has been used in some kind of ritualistic practice.' Or, The Endless *Conjuring* Universe," the sequels, prequels and other films of the so-called *Conjuring* Universe are analyzed in relationship to the original. The volume concludes with "What Exactly is Conjured in *The Conjuring*?" After all, if the film is called *The Conjuring*, something must have been summoned or some kind of magic has been wrought, and yet there is no literal conjuring in the film.

While the film has come under criticism, *The Conjuring* remains one of the best reviewed horror films of recent years, appearing on many horror critics' top ten lists. Its influence, for better or worse, is palpable and ongoing, yet little critical analysis has been written about it as of this writing. Tres Dean argues, "Wan's 2011-2013 double-whammy of *Insidious* and *The Conjuring* has defined the modern generation of mainstream horror. Whether this is a good or bad thing varies depending on who you ask" (Dean 2019). If you are asking me, it is a good but complicated thing. The purpose of this volume is to unpack this challenging and scary film, finding it to be an important one, not without its flaws, that has indeed defined modern popular horror and reinvented the ghost story for a mainstream audience.

SYNOPSIS

The Conjuring opens with Ed and Lorraine Warren (Patrick Wilson and Vera Farmiga) taking possession of the doll Annabelle, itself the conduit for a demon, from a pair of student nurses who had been terrified by the doll, and then transitions into a university lecture by the couple, establishing them as famous paranormal investigators. The film then introduces the Perron family, Roger and Carolyn (Ron Livingston and Lili Taylor) and their five daughters, who have moved into an old farmhouse in rural Rhode Island that was once the home of Bathsheba Sherman, a witch and child-murderer from the eighteenth century. Strange things begin to happen around the house, progressing in both intensity and terror until the Perrons are forced to seek out help from the

Warrens. Ed and Lorraine arrive at the house to discover several spirits haunting it, including Rory, a young boy killed by his mother when she was possessed by Bathsheba in the nineteenth century, all under the demonic influence of Bathsheba. The Warrens and their team investigate the home, experience the paranormal phenomena, and attempt to get permission from the Church for an exorcism. However, before receiving permission, Carolyn is possessed by Bathsheba and attempts to kill her two youngest daughters. Ed attempts an emergency exorcism and fails. Lorraine then appeals to the mother in Carolyn to fight Bathsheba, ending the possession and driving Bathsheba from the house for good. The film concludes with both the Perrons and Warrens safe, and the Warrens learning of a case in Long Island that needs their attention.

Chapter One: "It's right behind you!" or Rated R for "Terror"

Too Scary?

The Motion Picture Association of America (MPAA) rated *The Conjuring* "Restricted": "Rated R for sequences of disturbing violence and terror." The film contains no nudity, no sex, no gore, no extreme violence, no smoking and only a handful of expletives, yet still earned an R rating. While a PG-13 would possibly have allowed for more box office earnings, the film was released with an R for "terror" – for a film in which not a single character dies. Not one. That would seem to indicate that it is a rare horror film: one that relies upon different elements than gore, violence, and the depiction of death to create dread. Indeed, it gets its power from what it does not show. The scariest things in the film are arguably the things we, the audience, cannot see, but some of those in the film can.

Films are voluntarily submitted to the Classification and Rating Administration ("CARA") to be rated according to their five categories (G, PG, PG-13, R, NC-17). As stated in the MPAA's own guidelines:

> An R-rated motion picture, in the view of the Rating Board, contains some adult material. An R-rated motion picture may include adult themes, adult activity, hard language, intense or persistent violence, sexually-oriented nudity, drug abuse or other elements, so that parents are counseled to take this rating very seriously. Children under 17 are not allowed to attend R-rated motion pictures unaccompanied by a parent or adult guardian. Parents are strongly urged to find out more about R-rated motion pictures in determining their suitability for their children. Generally, it is not appropriate for parents to bring their young children with them to R-rated motion pictures. (MPAA 2010, 8)

The film's rating box, which appears both before any preview of that film as well as at the beginning of the film itself, lists the elements that led to that particular rating – which is, again, why it is remarkable that *The Conjuring*'s sole reason for being an R-rated picture is "disturbing violence and terror." There is no nudity, drug abuse, hard language, sexual content, or gore – only very scary images and concepts. The violence is not extreme, only "disturbing."

In response to this rating, Ian Buckwalter, writing in *The Atlantic*, critiqued the MPAA, noting that the organization is, "notoriously arbitrary and not prone to explaining their actions publicly" (2013). Having submitted the film to the MPAA, the producers were told, "there was nothing that could be altered in the film to get it to a PG-13" (2013). Buckwalter calls this, "the sort of publicity impresario William Castle would have killed for back in the '50s and '60s – 'the film deemed too scary for teens!'," and certainly the producers were happy to capitalize on this rating. Buckwalter asks, "Just how can terror be measured? [...] How do you quantify the subjective quality of fear?" His response: watch the movie in a theatre full of people, noting that when he did, "it seemed like the entire theatre was holding its breath. We were united in one feeling: terror." Thus, in an article entitled "Did *The Conjuring* Really Deserve an R Rating Just for Being Scary?," which seems to imply doubt, Buckwalter actually concludes, "the answer has to be yes," and proposes, "If the MPAA is looking for an objective standard for R-rated terror going forward, they might as well just add to the rating, 'as scary as *The Conjuring*.'" High praise indeed, and critical confirmation of the uniqueness of *The Conjuring* in twenty-first century horror cinema. It is a horror film that actually terrorizes its audience, not through gore or violence or jump scares (though it does use the last effectively), but through tension, dread, and implication.

H.P. Lovecraft opens his insightful *Supernatural Horror in Literature* by observing, "The oldest and strongest emotion of mankind is fear, and the oldest and strongest kind of fear is fear of the unknown" (1973, 12). *The Conjuring*, as will be argued below, exploits this idea to the hilt, frightening audiences by ensuring they often do not know what is actually happening. The most frightening moment in the entire film is a literal unknown – Christine seeing something behind Nancy, who insists, "There's nothing there." And, indeed, we can see nothing there. But there is clearly something there, as Christine can see it and whatever it is slams a door. *The Conjuring* is an exercise in creating fear of the unknown, which then transforms into fear of what we think we know, both terrifying the audience and earning an R rating for "terror."

"Terror," it should be noted, is the highest in Stephen King's taxonomy of horror. In his critical analysis of the cultural history of horror, *Danse Macabre*, King divides horror into three categories (1981). Better than the "gross out" or "horror," the first two categories, terror profoundly disturbs and is, "when you come home and notice everything you own had been taken away and replaced by an exact substitute. It's when the lights go out and you feel something behind you, you hear it, you feel its breath against your ear, but when you turn around, there's nothing there," as King summarized his own theory in a Facebook post in 2011. *The Conjuring* is an exercise in Terror with a capital T.

Three standout moments are mentioned a good deal in the criticism. This chapter analyzes all three in detail to show how *The Conjuring* delivers its horror. The first is the invisible thing in the bedroom, and the second involves Carolyn Perron standing at the top of the cellar stairs when hands come out of the darkness to clap, and the third and final is the hanged witch only Lorraine can see. In the first, the scariest moment in the film is rooted in the idea that the audience sees nothing. The characters see something, and what they experience and their reaction to it creates the horror. Wan preys upon the audience's fears by hiding the horror, sometimes in the shadows and darkness (where it is difficult to see), and sometimes in plain sight – you just can't see it.

The two middle Perron daughters, Nancy and Christine, share a room. Their relationship is depicted as typical sisters; sometimes friends, sometimes not, always overfamiliar with each other. Christine wakes up and, in a state of half sleep says, "Stop it, Nancy. It's not funny anymore." In a previous scene, also set at 3:07 in the morning, Christine had accused Nancy of getting out of bed and pulling her leg as a joke. Nancy denied doing it and was clearly in her own bed on the other side of the room. "I'm trying to sleep," Christine asserts this time. "Please stop grabbing my feet."

Her leg is pulled much more forcefully then by something not visible. Her body begins to be pulled across the bed and she springs fully awake, pulling her leg back and scrambling towards the headboard. She looks over at Nancy who is still asleep, facing away from her several feet away in her own bed. Her breathing becomes panicked, hyperventilating. She hears breathing and movement in the darkness of the room and it seems like something is moving under her bed. The camera follows her head over the foot of the bed to see if anything is there, but there is not. She sits on the bed for a moment and then begins to whimper as the camera follows her to look over the side of the bed.

The camera then alternates between a shot of her head hanging upside down looking under the bed and another showing her point-of-view, scanning across the floor in the darkness to see if anything is in the room. It is a shot we have seen many times before, to varying degrees of effectiveness – a child looking for something under their bed. Audiences have been trained to think that there will either be something lurking, as in *Lights Out* (2016, David F. Sandberg), or that the child will look under the bed, find nothing, and come back up to the top of the bed where the monster will be waiting, as is the case with the clown doll in *Poltergeist* (1982, Tobe Hooper). Indeed, the "monster under the bed trope" will be employed most effectively in *Annabelle: Creation* (2017, David F. Sandberg). Wan very cleverly relies upon the trope to create tension – first by the slow travel of Christine's head down to look under the bed, building suspense, and then the reveal that there is nothing under the bed, which immediately prepares the audience for the jump scare when she comes back up; Wan ratchets up the tension by having nothing on the topside of the bed waiting for her (and us).

The camera then zooms in on her face as we hear the door creaking open, continuing the slow build of tension. The audience now does not know where the threat will come from as Wan has shown the old tropes will not be employed here except to manipulate you into thinking they might be. The soundtrack carries her heartbeat, beginning to pound, as the camera follows her, turning with her to face the door, which is slowly opening. The effect is disorienting and adds to the suspense of the scene. The camera then again alternates between slowly zooming in on a terrified Christine and a shot just over her shoulder of what she is seeing – a patch of darkness behind the door. Nothing is visible to the audience, yet she is clearly seeing something and beginning to panic. It bears repeating: there is nothing visible under the bed, on top of the bed, or behind the door, yet the tension is as high as it can go. Wan holds onto Lovecraft's fear of the unknown for as long as possible without going for the obvious and immediate jump scare.

Christine calls Nancy's name in a terrified voice until her sister wakes up. "What are you doing?" asks Nancy. Seeing Christine sitting cross-legged on her bed staring into the dark, Nancy realizes something is wrong and puts on her glasses. "Are you all right?" she asks her sister.

"Do you see it?" asks Christine, never taking her eyes off what she sees.

THE CONJURING

"It's looking right at us." – Christine can see what the audience, and Nancy, cannot.

The audience looks over Christine's shoulder at Nancy – "It's standing right behind you."

At this point I applaud Wan. The audience is dying to see what it is. We know Christine is seeing something terrifying. We are watching a horror movie, so we want to see what she sees. Then Wan pulls a magic trick (or at least the misdirection before the trick). The camera moves from viewing Christine and Nancy in bed to looking over Christine's shoulder (with Nancy still in the shot) at the darkness behind the door. "See what?" asks Nancy.

Pointing, Christine says in a broken voice, "There's someone behind the door."

"What?" Nancy feels Christine's fear, but is also confused – she sees nothing.

"There's someone standing over there." The genius of this moment is that while it is obvious Christine is terrified out of her wits, neither Nancy nor the audience can see what she is seeing. "It's looking right at us," Christine tells her.

Let's look at this language. Christine says "it." Not "she," not "he", but "it." What she is seeing is somehow indescribable or at the very least not human. Nancy cannot see it, nor can the audience. It, however, can see us. It is looking right at us. Based on the camera POV, we are now with Christine – "it" is looking at her and us. Again, the genius is the simplicity of it. The tension has now been held for over a minute as the audience waits for Wan to reveal what "it" is. Now, however, the audience knows that whatever Christine is seeing, it is looking at us. The effect is uncanny and unsettling.

Nancy walks over quickly, despite Christine begging her not to. "There's no one here, see?" she says, waving her hand through the darkness and moving the door. "Ugh," she then says. "It's that smell again." As the real Ed and Lorraine Warren would note, as do their cinematic doppelgängers, this smell is a sign of the supernatural evil of the house itself. The smell is a marker of the presence of supernatural evil. It lurks in the wardrobe and in the darkness, it only comes at night, and it smells terrible; the entity in the house assaults the senses in order to terrify and threaten the Perrons and, by extension, the audience. Though we cannot smell the horrific smell, it is enough the characters on screen do.

Cut to a reverse shot of Christine, eyes filled with tears, creating an eerie effect. Moonlight is coming through the window, illuminating both the white-painted parts of the window and reflecting off Christine's black hair. It also has the effect of making her tear-filled eyes seem like they are supernaturally glowing. "Oh, my God," she whispers. The camera is now back to the POV behind her shoulder; Nancy is framed by darkness, the only light coming from the hall, reflecting off the door and illuminating her left side. "It's standing right behind you," Christine whispers.

As Nancy slowly turns to look, the door slams shut, plunging the room into darkness.

Let's take a moment to unpack how this scare is easily the most effective in the film. First, the entire sequence lasts about 75 seconds of sustained tension. From the first moment the sheet is pulled off Christine to the slam of the door, there is no break or release. Wan shows the reaction first – Christine is clearly terrified. The audience understands how to read the moment from her reaction. The normal film pattern is event, and then reaction shot. Wan gives a reaction with no visible event. He thus violates a number of tropes, from the looking-under-the-bed trope to the idea that the reaction to something takes places after we see that something, creating further tension in the audience. The film then shows the audience, frankly, nothing. Nancy stands in the darkness and the film has shown us there is definitely something there we cannot see. The scary thing that is most definitely there, and we cannot see it. Because we cannot see it, it can get us. That, in turn, makes this moment one of the most terrifying in the film.

To close out the scene, the rest of the family comes running at the girls' screams. It is clear both are upset, but Christine is mad with fear. She insists there was someone in the room with them. Roger acts like a concerned parent, believing there might have been an actual person in the room, but once he looks around the room he assures his daughter with confidence that it was "just a bad dream." Then the other shoe drops. "It talked to me," Christine tells them, shaking her head. "It said that it wants my family dead." Wan immediately cuts to a reaction shot of Nancy, Cindy and Andrea, all looking concerned for Christine, but also now uncertain of what is going on. The family is clearly being threatened and it is obvious to all except Roger that something serious and possibly supernatural is happening in the house. The denouement of the scene provides an appropriate coda to the tension Wan built in the first minute and a half. The door slam was the jump scare to put a full stop on the tension that had been built, and now a new, underlying tension has been laid. Christine's warning begins to build the dread again. It is a masterful sequence that inspires fear, dread and a jump.

Further proof that this segment is very effective is found in the following scene, when we do actually get to see something – Bathsheba on top of Andrea's closet. It is startling, and a wonderful jump scare moment. Bathsheba Sherman, the demonic murderous witch into whose farmhouse the Perrons have moved, has manifested for the first time on screen at this moment. She is truly malevolent and creepy-looking as played by Joseph Bishara, the film's composer. But the moment in no way inspires the terror of nothing in the dark from the previous scene. In fact, the visual of Bathsheba on top of the wardrobe is only as effective as it is because the scene with Nancy and Christine has now primed the audience for supernatural horror.

Bathsheba Sherman revealed atop Andrea's wardrobe.

The second key moment comes a night or two after the terror in the girl's bedroom. Roger is presumably out on the road, and Carolyn is home alone with the girls. She is in the bathroom and has another bruise. She takes iron pills that a doctor has clearly prescribed in response to her large number of unexplained bruises. Betsy Brye's "Sleep Walk" underscores the scene, and then transfers to the radio that Carolyn listens to as she folds the laundry. A 1959 hit for Brye (real name: Bette Anne Steele), the song is sung by a sleepwalking woman missing her lover, whom apparently she wronged, and as a result can no longer dream while asleep. Wan sets a standard domestic scene: mom folding laundry while quietly listening to music as the kids sleep. She hears the girls giggling and turns off the radio. She then hears the twin claps of someone playing Hide-and-Clap. Again, thus far in the film we have seen nothing. In the previous scene the audience saw Christine see something. Now we, too, are beginning to hear noises coming from elsewhere in the house. Again, this is a standard technique in horror films.

Carolyn goes to investigate. She checks the girls in their various bedrooms and they are all asleep. She looks downstairs from the landing at the top of the stairs. The grandfather clock in the hall is very loud. As she checks Andrea's room, she hears a series of loud crashes, glass breaking and a girl giggling. Running back to the landing, Carolyn (and the audience) sees that all of the family photos on the wall lining the stairs have been knocked off and thrown to the ground. The stairs are covered in glass.

Carolyn carefully moves downstairs to survey the damage and see if the person who caused it is around. She again hears two claps from the back of the house. She walks past the basement door and turns on a light in the study. She then looks in the kitchen and hears the sound of a door creaking. The camera shows that the cellar door is open and we hear the sound of the discordant piano playing. Carolyn enters the top of the stairs.

What follows is a shot looking up at her from the darkness. The lightbulb above her is the only source of light. The cellar is pitch-black. As in the scene with Christine, we have a single character, lit in a dim pool of light, surrounded by darkness; the screen cuts to a reverse angle, from behind Carolyn's right shoulder, looking down into the pitch-black cellar. She turns on the cellar lights and takes a step or two down the stairs. She looks around — nothing out of the ordinary. "Who's ever down there, I'm gonna lock you in now." She still thinks (hopes?) it is a human intruder. She knows it cannot be one of the girls, she just saw all of them asleep. Then we get the first jump scare of the scene. The cellar door slams shut, knocking her down the stairs. She lands heavy on the cement floor.

She takes her time getting up, with ominous underscoring hinting that the ordeal is not over but rather is only now beginning. Thus far the situation has been strange, but now it contains a genuine threat. It is clear from Lili Taylor's performance Carolyn is injured and groggy. Behind her, in the background, the cellar is a hodgepodge of furniture, sheets covering things, piles of junk. Anything could be hiding in the mess and would be hard to spot. The audience (especially those who have seen and learned from the earlier films *Paranormal Activity* and *Insidious*) begins scanning the background. A single bulb burns in the center of the room.

The film cuts to a close-up of Carolyn. Her face is bruised and she is deeply shaken. What initially seems to be her POV scan of the room suddenly finds her on the left of the screen, the room unfolding in front of her. Out of the pile of junk, a ball comes flying and bounces towards her, sending her upstairs in a panic as both lightbulbs shatter, leaving the cellar (and the theatre) in darkness as we hear the girl giggle again.

In the dark we hear matches striking and one flares up to reveal the camera partway down the stairs, pointing up at Carolyn, who is surrounded by darkness. Her hand trembles as she holds the match in front of her. A reverse angle behind Carolyn shows her looking down the stairs – the flickering match casting as many shadows as weak light

Lorraine sees what we, and Ed, cannot.

into the cellar. The match burns out and again Carolyn (and the audience) is plunged into darkness. She lights a second match. A girl's voice says, "Hey, wanna play hide-and-clap?" She focuses on the bottom of the stairs and out of the darkness to her right comes a pair of hands that clap twice. The lights go out. In the darkness, Carolyn pounds on the door as the girls sleep.

The pair of hands coming out of the dark to clap is an expected jump scare and is very well set up. However, they also literally embody the sense of the uncanny that has been building from the beginning of the film. Emerging out of the dark, they are not connected to a visible body, which makes them abject and uncanny. The hands are grey with black nails. They are adult hands. We know this is not Rory or some other child ghost playing a prank, this is something else, something malevolent using a child's game to terrify Carolyn. Wan has very carefully set up the entire moment from the instant we first see the children playing Hide-and-Clap, but now it is the adults who are playing (see chapter three for more on this).

The third key moment arrives with Ed and Lorraine as they appear at the house for the first time. After meeting the Perrons and seeing the ghost of young Rory reflected in the music box, Lorraine exits into the backyard and strolls out to the twisted tree by the water. As she walks under the tree, Wan uses a wide shot, making her seem small compared to the house and the tree. Lorraine is isolated in and dominated by the landscape in which she appears. The film then cuts to her point of view: the dock, the

Bathsheba Sherman, hanged — but seen only by Lorraine.

water, a canoe tied up. Sunlight streams down on a beautiful fall day. It seems like a lovely rural scene.

Ed exits the house and looks for her. Again, the long shot of the two of them, the malformed tree and the house behind them dwarfing the Warrens, a visual reminder of the size of the horror they are up against, even though it appears to be unseen at the moment. "Hey," Ed says in greeting. We then hear a rope stretched taut, as if something heavy were hanging from it. Close up on Lorraine, growing fearful. She turns and looks at Ed. The camera pans to Ed, who asks, "What is it?" A reverse angle shot follows, showing Lorraine looking at something just above and behind Ed's head. She shrinks down and the shot is from over Ed's shoulder, so whatever she is looking at dominates her. The rope sound intensifies. Wan cuts back to the previous shot of Ed, but now visible are two dirty grey feet and the bottom of a nightgown, clearly a hanged body. The toes are black, the legs and feet skeletal and mottled grey. Ed cannot see or hear it, only Lorraine and the audience. Reverse angle again and Lorraine looks up at the face of whatever it is and grows even more fearful. Ed turns and looks behind him but sees nothing. The film doesn't show what she sees, but it is clearly terrifying, and she begins to faint.

All three of these scenes are within the first hour of the film. The first half sets up the horrifying reality of the Perron house. It is a slow build, but effective. By the time Lorraine sees the hanged body of Bathsheba, Wan has created sustained tension and dread, as well as established the reality of the haunting. That the Perron house is the site of supernatural events is never in doubt. That Ed and Lorraine Warren are warriors against malevolent entities is likewise a given. The second half of the film then is the investigation, exorcism and eventual defeat of Bathsheba and her demonic cohort.

All three scenes evoke sustained anxiety in the audience. We know something is happening or about to happen, but we do not know what. It is less the minimal "violence" of the film, as the anxiety maintained throughout that (far more than the jump scares) leave the audience afraid. What is also remarkable about this is that the film relies very little on digital effects and realizes most of its special effects in-camera. Critics praised the period designs, the performances, the score and the overall structure of the film as transforming a simple story into a horror masterpiece. *Variety* called it, "a sensationally entertaining old-school freakout and one of the smartest, most viscerally effective thrillers in recent memory" (Chang 2013, 88). Indeed, nostalgia and the feeling of the film being an "old-school freakout" contributed greatly to the film's appeal and success. Not only is the film set in the seventies, it evokes and echoes the great horror films of that decade: *The Exorcist*, *The Wicker Man* (1973, Robin Hardy), *The Legend of Hell House* (1973, John Hough), *The Texas Chainsaw Massacre* (1974, Tobe Hooper), *The Omen* (1976, Richard Donner), *Halloween* (1978, John Carpenter), *Phantasm* (1979, Don Coscarelli), and *The Amityville Horror*. *The Conjuring* relies neither on gross-out horror nor an abundance of jump scares (although it does have its share of them).

The phenomena continued through the *Conjuring* films. *The Conjuring 2* (2016, James Wan) is rated R for "Terror and Horror Violence." *Annabelle* (2014, John R. Leonetti) is rated R for "for intense sequences of disturbing violence and terror." *Annabelle: Creation* is Rated R for "horror violence and terror." *The Nun* (2018, Corin Hardy) is rated R "for terror, violence, and disturbing/bloody images." *The Curse of La Llorona* is rated R "for violence and terror." The films were regarded slightly differently in the UK. All *Conjuring* Universe films to date have been rated 15 by the British Board of Film Classification for "strong horror," or "strong supernatural threat, horror, injury detail." The 15 rating means *The Conjuring* films can be seen unaccompanied by a slightly younger group than in the United States (15 as opposed to 17). Note, however, that the reason for the rating remains the same: horror, supernatural threat, and "injury detail," which I assume refers to the harm that seemingly comes to Carolyn while possessed in the basement, as there are no other significant injuries in the film.

Another of the aspects that makes the film effective is that Wan and his screenwriters slowly build up the worlds and lives of the Warrens and the Perrons. The Perron children are all sharply drawn, and the situations of the adults in both families are clearly defined and demonstrate an increasing threat to each family unit. We care about them and thus there is more at stake for the audience when the supernatural events begin to occur. Wan pulls strong performances out of his actors. The "monster" is scary – Bathsheba, like the shark in *Jaws* (1975, Steven Spielberg), is kept off-screen for much of the film. In other words, *The Conjuring* creates empathetic characters; the audience is invested in them and their confrontation with a terrifying unknown that, as we slowly learn what it is and what it wants, loses nothing of its ability to scare. In short, as Tomris Laffly brilliantly summarized in a review of *The Conjuring 2*, the original film "summoned and devilishly exploited (as a good horror film should) the underlying anxieties of the vulnerable everyman: not only around real-life hurdles of parenthood and financial hardship, but also the unknown, unseen and haunting traces the sorrow of others leaves through time" (2016).

JAMES WAN, ARCH-CONJURER, AND HIS MAGICIAN'S ASSISTANTS

"Conjuring" implies a conjurer – someone who works the magic to make something appear. Credit where credit is due: A.A. Dowd writes that "the true star of *The Conjuring*... [is] the man on the other side of the camera" (2013). James Wan is an Australian producer, screenwriter and director of Malaysian Chinese descent who has sat at the helm for the launch of not one but three horror franchises: *Saw*, *Insidious* and *The Conjuring*, all three of which have produced multiple sequels and prequels, proving profoundly influential on the genre. As of this writing, Wan has directed ten feature length films, seven of which are horror and the other three are action (*Death Sentence* [2007], *Furious 7* [2015] and *Aquaman* [2018]). He has also directed several short films and some television episodes. He is slated to direct another half dozen films (including an additional sequel to *Insidious* and a sequel to *Aquaman*) over the next few years.

Stygian (2000), Wan's first film as a director, is an Australian horror film in which a young couple find themselves trapped in another world called "Exile." It is also his only Australian film to date. For his next project, Wan and screenwriting partner Leigh

Whannell had created a short film featuring Whannell in a "bear trap" head device as a calling card to get funding for a full-length feature. That film, *Saw*, produced in the United States, premiered to critical acclaim at Sundance in 2004, generating a span of sequels, from *Saw II* (2005, Darren Lynn Bousman) to *Spiral* (2021, Darren Lynn Bousman) with six more films in between those two.

Saw is extreme horror and is viewed by many as the film that marks the birth of so-called torture porn, bringing the film series a good deal of criticism. Yet Benjamin Poole argues that the influence of *Saw* spreads beyond that specific subgenre, being echoed in mainstream films such as *Casino Royale* (2006, Martin Campbell) and *The Dark Knight* (2008, Christopher Nolan), both of which present scenes of torture and prisoner-dilemma situations (2012, 16). I have also argued elsewhere that the *Saw* films, like other torture porn, can be read as an attempt by the United States to come to terms with the fact that it was torturing people in Iraq, Guantanamo and other so-called "black sites" and third-party locations, and the nation's ambiguous feelings about torture, leading to narratives that seemingly justified it (Wetmore 2012).

Wan's next major feature was 2007s *Dead Silence*, which carries with it a number of elements found in Wan's later horror films. The film tells the story of Jamie Ashen, who fled his cursed hometown only to return when his new bride is murdered mysteriously. His investigations uncover the dark secret of Raven's Fair: in the 1940s a famous ventriloquist named Mary Shaw was falsely accused of kidnapping a local boy and was killed by a lynch mob and buried with her dummies. Her spirit since has been killing the families of those involved in her murder. At heart, the film, like *The Conjuring*, is a mystery, an attempt to uncover why a woman is haunting (and harming) the people of this small town. Mary Shaw is a female monster, not unlike Bathsheba Sherman, manipulating the events and the characters behind the scenes. As with *Saw*, the ending reveals that the audience has been tricked into thinking they know what happened. Instead, the film reveals that Jamie's parents, and several other "people" in the town, were not alive when Jamie interacted with them – they were hollowed-out corpses used as ventriloquist dummies. The cinematography is similar to *The Conjuring*: interplay of light and dark with malevolent things hidden in the shadows, washed out color, and a moving camera. Like *The Conjuring*, Wan creates a slow build of dread combined with jump scares. Mary's primary ventriloquist dummy, Billy, seems to have a life of its own. The film begins with

Jamie and his wife opening a mysterious package with Billy inside, despite the fact that, as the audience learns later, the doll had been buried with Mary Shaw. Re-watching *Dead Silence* after *The Conjuring*, one can see the seeds of Annabelle being laid. Billy's face is carved wood, and shares Annabelle's sinister features and stare. The film begins with a disturbing doll with an uncanny history. Wan knows how to make inanimate toys eerie and unsettling.

That same year saw the release of Wan's fourth film, *Death Sentence*, an action thriller with horror elements. The film concerns a business executive whose family is attacked as part of a gang initiation ritual. Based on the novel *Death Sentence* (a direct sequel to *Death Wish* by Brian Garfield, previously made into a film with Charles Bronson in 1974), the film depicts the executive, played by Kevin Bacon, hunting down and killing the men who attacked his family.

Wan's fifth and seventh films, bookending *The Conjuring*, are the first two *Insidious* films (2011, 2013). As with *Dead Silence*, *Insidious* also has many elements in common with *The Conjuring* (not least the presence in both of Patrick Wilson). The Lambert family moves into an old house, in which some odd things seem to begin happening. Then Dalton, the oldest son, falls off a ladder in the attic and seems to go into a coma, which exacerbates the odd events. Eventually the family, believing they are living in a haunted house, move. The strange events continue to occur, until the grandmother sees a hideous monster in the kitchen and psychic Elise Ranier (played by Lin Shaye and who will become the central figure in the *Insidious* universe, despite being killed in the first film) is brought in to help identify the evil plaguing the family. She reveals Dalton has been astrally projecting, traveling out of his body, which makes it appealing to entities that would possess and take over the body so that they might have an incarnate existence. The boy is being held in a supernatural realm called "the further," a place which his father, when he was a boy, also used to be able to travel to, leaving him under threat from the malevolent ghost of a woman in black. A demonic being behind a haunting, a family mysteriously subjected to the supernatural, the entrance of a psychically gifted woman who might be able to end the unearthly upheaval, and the presence of comic sidekick paranormal investigators are all elements from *Insidious* that will repeat in *The Conjuring*. *Insidious 2* continues and expands the story.

Wan has consistently demonstrated his own ability to work as a director at all levels, from low-budget independent films to Hollywood blockbusters, and is clearly comfortable working in genre, especially in action and horror. He is a stylist and his craft is on full display with *The Conjuring*. Long takes, moving handheld cameras following characters, blurred focus, cavernous pools of darkness, unnerving camera angles, masterful use of light and darkness: the whole is greater than the sum of the filmmaking parts. Wan-as-magician is also a master of misdirection, setting up what seems to be a jump scare and instead delivering something more. Even better than his jump scares is his narrative misdirection. Wan tells the audience to look over here, and then pulls off the trick – in magic, this is called misdirection. This technique pays off in *The Conjuring*, which seems like a topper for *Insidious*, also an effective haunted-house-that-is-more-than-a-haunted-house-story, but one not as purely rendered as in *The Conjuring*.

The screenplay was written by Chad and Carey Hayes, twin brothers who also wrote a number of television episodes for various series, the script for the 2005 remake of *House of Wax* (Jaume Collet-Serra), as well as the screenplay for *The Reaping* (2007, Stephen Hopkins), another theological horror film in which a former missionary-turned-scientist who specializes in debunking religious phenomena encounters the demonic and the divine in a small Louisiana town called Haven. The brothers Hayes have an obvious interest in religious horror and how films designed to scare can also be films about faith. This issue will be explored in much greater depth in the next chapter.

In order to effect the magic tricks, Wan had a number of his usual magician's assistants who are invested in the larger *Conjuring* universe. One thing to note is that Wan often attempts to collaborate with the same production team, as they are able to work with him in a manner which brings his vision to fruition. Director of Photography John R. Leonetti had previously worked with Wan on *Dead Silence* and *Insidious*. He went on co-produce *Insidious Chapter 2* (2013, James Wan) and direct *Annabelle* (2014). He filmed *The Conjuring* using Arri Alexa, Leica Summilux-C and Fujinon Premier Lenses, lighting for a washed out look that captured a sense of the period setting and creating a world of both black and white and also muted colors. Production designer Julie Berghoff (who also performed the same duties on *Saw*, *Dead Silence* and *Death Sentence* with Wan) created masterful sets and spaces. The farmhouse and the Warren's occult museum are as much characters as the people in this film and Berghoff deserves credit for creating a world in which the events of *The Conjuring* seem plausible.

As much as the visuals, the soundscape of the film adds to the terror. The sound design is by Joe Dzuban, who also worked on *Insidious Chapter 2*, *Annabelle* and on Wan's *Aquaman* (2018) as sound designer, as well as supervising sound editor on *The Conjuring 2*. Joseph Bishara, who scored the film, frequently collaborates with Wan both as composer and as a performer (he plays Bathsheba Sherman in *The Conjuring* and the Lipstick-Faced demon in *Insidious*). Bishara's score is eerie and evocative. Brass, strings, wind, piano and harp are the key instruments for his compositions for the film (Fichera 2016, 62). It is the brass that he uses to particular effect, especially low notes that decrescendo. Bishara creates both layered dissonance and a tension broken by startling sounds – softly played sections, followed by the aural equivalent of the jump scare. As one reviewer of the soundtrack observed:

> Bishara can warp white noise to be vicious and foreboding and manipulates the droning negative space around the track's harsh shrieking mid-sections into uneasy and suffocating forms. He also toys around with the idea of distance in the compositions on *The Conjuring*, as tracks will either approach listeners from afar, surround and engulf them, or remain disturbingly complacent until they jarringly shift into a more violent tone. (breakingthefragile, 2013)

The critic is correct, and it should be noted that the musical distance created by the compositions, especially through the use of brass work equally with the visuals of the film to maintain an element of dread that is simultaneously distant and getting closer. Bishara also relies upon an instrument called a "rust piano" to create dissonant and jarring sounds as part of the soundtrack. The "rust piano" is literally the remains of a rusted, rotted old piano Bishara found in an alley and uses to produce the distinctive sounds in his horror soundtracks, most effectively in *The Conjuring*.

The same reviewer notes that the music adds to the scares by creating an audio landscape that "suit[s] the tone of the film and feel[s] like a lengthy process of conjuring, as all the sounds lethargically gather together and collect into a pool of swirling anxiety before Bishara keeps listeners guessing by either striking them with a climactic jump scare, or sometimes just simply leaving them waiting for it, and its inconsistencies like that that maintains the score's shroud of uncertainty" (breakingthefragile, 2013). The key word here is "conjuring." The score, like the film, is a "lengthy process of conjuring," summoning something from the depths that perhaps we do not want to see.

PRODUCTION

Texas-based producer Tony DeRosa-Grund had written a treatment for a film he called *The Conjuring* after Ed Warren played him a recording from the Perron investigation. After almost two decades of no interest from film studios, he attempted to produce the film with Gold Circle Films, which had produced *The Haunting in Connecticut*. Interestingly, *The Haunting in Connecticut* concerned another case in which the Warrens were called in to consult. They are present in the Discovery Channel series *A Haunting*, which featured an episode entitled "A Haunting in Connecticut." In 1986, the Snedeker family had moved into a home in Southington, Connecticut to be close to son Stephen's cancer treatments. When strange phenomena, including apparitions, began occurring, the Warrens were called in and claimed the home had been a former funeral home at which the morticians had also carried out satanic rituals. With writer Ray Garton, Carmen and Al Snedeker and the Warrens published *In a Dark Place: The True Story of a Haunting* in 1992, which allegedly narrates the entire experience the Snedeker family had in the Southington Home. Garton later claimed that Ed Warren told him, "You've got some of the story — just use what works and make the rest up… Just make it up and make it scary" (Radford 2009). Nevertheless, the Snedeker family's story then became the basis for *The Haunting in Connecticut*, which takes the basic tale (a family moves into a mortuary and is haunted) and replaces the Warrens with "Reverend Nicholas Popescu," a composite character and ghost hunter/exorcist played by Elias Koteas. As with *The Conjuring*, the label "based on a true story" proved controversial for *The Haunting in Connecticut*, which will be explored in more depth in the next chapter.

Unable to secure a deal with Gold Circle Films, DeRosa-Grund joined with producer Peter Safran and the brothers Hayes, who wrote a screenplay based on DeRosa-Grund's treatment, focusing more on the Warrens. Eventually six studios began bidding on the script, with Summit Entertainment first signing onto produce, but when the deal stalled New Line Features picked up the project (Andreeva 2013). James Wan, who at the time had found success with *Insidious*, claimed to be more interested in the "based on a true story" aspect of the project than in telling another ghost story (Collis 2013). New Line was impressed with the success of *Insidious*, and Wan stated, "I knew I wanted to get back into the studio filmmaking system and I felt that basically making a movie that's similar to the world that I came from would make the studio feel comfortable giving me the chance to do it" (Collis 2013). With Wan signed on, casting began in January of 2012; the four principals, Patrick Wilson (Ed Warren), Vera Farmiga (Lorraine Warren), Lili Taylor (Carolyn Perron) and Ron Livingston (Roger Perron), were brought into preproduction almost immediately.

Principal photography was carried out in and around Wilmington and Currie, North Carolina from February 22 to 26 April 2012 on a twenty-million-dollar budget. One presumes the choice of location was both for the budget (it being less expensive to film in North Carolina than New England) and for the weather – from February through April most of New England is very obviously in the grips of winter, frequently with snow. The challenge (especially for native New Englanders such as this author) is that the film is set in late October through November in Rhode Island, which looks nothing like North Carolina in spring. In early scenes it is obviously not fall, as the trees are denuded and green buds have begun to form that will grow into leaves. A quick review of the exterior scenes show spring, not fall, is the season. While this does not take away from the film or its horror, it is nevertheless interesting that the location of the production resulted in a film with a narrative set in the autumn but with visual elements that depict the spring.

The film went into postproduction in August 2012 and was submitted for test screenings in the fall. Wan claims he cut between twenty and thirty minutes from the film between the initial edit and the final edit, that the test screenings were "incredibly positive," and that he knew before it was released that *The Conjuring* would be a hit (Weintraub 2013). New Line and Warner Brothers began marketing and promotion in November 2012, followed by an intense marketing campaign beginning the following February.

In the wake of the success of *The Conjuring*, Wan launched his own production company, Atomic Monster, on 21 October 2014. Thus far, Atomic Monster has produced *Annabelle* and all subsequent *Conjuring* universe films as well as *Lights Out*, directed by David S. Sandberg, who also directed *Annabelle: Creation*. Atomic Monster has several more films and television series currently in development, which seems to imply that *The Conjuring* has turned into the gift that keeps giving to the horror genre.

HUMOR

It is not merely in the technical aspects Wan and his collaborators work to construct a film rated R for "terror." It is in the direction of the performances and the humor of the script that audiences find mitigating moments that heighten the scares when they come. Wan employs humor expertly in the film, sometimes to humanize, as in when Ed asks Lorraine not to join him on an investigation and she responds by asking him, "Do you remember what you said to me on our wedding night?" He ponders for a moment and then says, "'Can we do it again?'" She looks at him coolly, then smiles and says, "After that." It's a lovely moment between two serious people who can be not fully serious with one another because of their relationship.

In a later scene, Ed tells Roger he is standing under the branch Bathsheba hanged herself from. Roger looks up and then slowly moves out from under it. Again: a nice human moment.

After the three scares described above, the investigatory team begins their occupation of the Perron house. Drew and Ed are in the study and Carolyn and Lorraine are in the living room when they all hear a bell ring. They had hung bells on all the doors so as to hear them open. In a long shot running over Carolyn and Lorraine's shoulders, we see Roger in the kitchen, then a door in the hallway slowly opens. It is actually the door right next to the cellar door, the downstairs bathroom. Officer Brad slowly exits the bathroom, walking backwards into the hallway, wiping his hands on a towel as we hear the sound of a toilet flushing. He notices everyone looking at him with trepidation. "What? I had to go!" he tells them as they relax. It is a wonderful moment on film as Wan has already created expectations that when we hear noises and a door or an item of furniture begins to move, we are about to witness a supernatural event that is designed to be terrifying. Brad unapologetically using the bathroom is a humorous deflation of this trope Wan has already employed several times in the film. The technique is simple. We have seen it before, and often. But that is what makes *The*

Conjuring so effective – not that it is breaking new ground, but that we are watching a virtuoso creation of a haunted house movie that "does it right."

SEEING (IS BELIEVING?) AND NOT SEEING

A last major theme that Wan also employs effectively to advance the horror is one that has already been explored in this chapter: that what you cannot see is terrifying. *The Conjuring* explores the idea of seeing as believing and not seeing as believing as well, as the eyes can be fooled; this is also in keeping with the idea of *The Conjuring* as a magic trick, an illusion. *The Conjuring* tells its characters and its audience not to trust their eyes, something that is ironic given that cinema is a visual medium.

"Do you want to see him?" April asks her mother, speaking of Rory.

"Yeah. How?" is Carolyn's response.

"With this. When the music stops you see him in the mirror standing behind you."

Carolyn stares intently into the music box mirror as the tune winds down. The music is creepy, the spiral pattern unsettling. When the music finally stops, April jumps into the frame in the mirror and yells "boo." April does the same thing the film does – tells the audience they are going to see something and then creates tension that is exploded with a jump scare, yet still nothing is seen.

The girls have seen and experienced things in the house, yet Roger cannot see what is going on. "It's just a bad dream," he insists, refusing to see the possibility of a genuine supernatural experience. He resists the evidence of others' eyes and refuses to take their word for it. On the horrific night when Carolyn is locked in the cellar during a game of Hide-and-Clap with whatever entity is in the house and the girls are attacked by Bathsheba, Roger runs in and can only stand demanding, "What's going on here?" He does not see, in all senses of the word. He does not visually see the ghosts, but he also does not understand what his family is experiencing, reminiscent of the proverb that there are none so blind as those who cannot see.

In the first example, cited above, Nancy cannot see what Christine can. Christine is more terrified because she can see; the audience, however, is terrified because Christine

Carolyn looks to see Rory's ghost in the music box lid.

can see what we cannot. Hide-and-Clap involves the voluntary loss of sight. The person who is "it" must wear a blindfold while searching for the other players. In a new house, where the layout is unfamiliar and furniture and unpacked boxes lie everywhere, this can prove especially challenging. In the two instances where we see actual games being played, this loss of sight proves injurious. Christine bumps into boxes and has to reassure her mother, "I'm okay. I'm okay." Yet it is clear the impact hurt. Similarly, when Carolyn agrees to play with April while the older girls are off at school, she bumps into a table in the hall, the bannister and balustrade on the landing upstairs, and the doorframe. When you voluntarily cannot see, the film seems to suggest, you will get hurt.

The Warrens enter the Perron house and what is terrifying to the women of the house and confusing to Roger is clear to the Warrens. Lorraine can see the entity hovering about the family, visualized for the audience as a black, smoky presence. Lorraine can see the hanged body of Bathsheba Sherman, as noted above. Ed cannot see it but believes that Lorraine can. It is only when the Warrens begin explaining and reassuring that Roger comes to understand and accept what he cannot see himself, and when he can he experiences the horrors that the rest of his family already has, culminating in the exorcism in the cellar. Hence the proverb, some things have to be seen to be believed, and some things have to be believed to be seen.

All of this seems to suggest that the true horror of *The Conjuring* is neither a haunting, nor a possession, but something ontological and epistemological: one can only fight

Carolyn willingly blindfolding herself to play "Hide and Clap," a metaphor for the willful blindness of the family ignoring the evil in the house.

the terrifying unknown if one believes it exists, and if one believes in something to counter it. In that sense, it is not merely a well-done scary movie, but, like *The Exorcist*, it approaches an existential fear – what is real? If the forces of darkness exist, then does God? And if so, what should we believe? This horror of *The Conjuring* is not the fear of the horror holy trinity of Freddie, Michael and Jason, but the very fear and trembling with which we approach ultimate (and everyday) reality. How do we know what we see is real? And how do we know there is not anything lurking that we cannot see, but that will horrify use once we experience it?

It is as a result of all of these elements coming together that I agree with critic Alonso Duralde: "*The Conjuring* scared me more than any other movie in recent memory" (2013). He concludes, "Most thrillers stop being terrifying when their mysteries are revealed, but in the screenplay by Chad Hayes and Carey Hayes, the more we know, the more we dread." *The Conjuring* is an effective horror film because it does not rely on gross outs, jump scares or hiding its horror. Arch-conjurer Wan and his magician's assistants build slow scenes rooted in a growing dread and sense of the uncanny that does not abate simply because we have a better sense of what is happening. The secret of *The Conjuring* is that the magic trick never stops – it continues throughout the film, until the audience scans the screen waiting for the next thing to happen.

Chapter Two: The Warren Files, or "Based on a True Story"

Much of the horror of *The Conjuring* has been ascribed to the idea that it is a "true story" and shows things that supposedly happened. Unlike other horror films, which are fictional and make no pretense to recount genuine reality, *The Conjuring* narrates a story that is "real." The Perrons, the Warrens and Bathsheba Sherman are and were real people. The film purports to depict a reality; its events are not only possible, they actually happened. The film is based entirely on authentic, tangible, factual experiences; the phenomena represented in it are part of a larger cultural continuum of paranormal investigation. The film is firmly rooted in Roman Catholic theology and spirituality and links its haunting to the actual history of witchcraft paranoia in colonial New England. In other words, the film is rooted in a number of different cultural realities and attempts to provoke fear through asserting itself as "real" and "true." The film, however, is also controversial for a number of reasons related to those truth claims.

Ed and Lorraine Warren are arguably best known (and certainly have spent the longest time in the public eye) as paranormal investigators. They were involved in the historic Amityville Horror case (disputed as a hoax), involved in the *Haunting in Connecticut / Snedeker* case (disputed as a hoax), investigated West Point for ghosts, participated in numerous exorcisms (disputed as hoaxes), and conducted hundreds of investigations of alleged hauntings. Numerous books have been written by and about them, and those books have been adapted into films and television episodes as well. But *The Conjuring* and its sequels represent the first attempt to construct this couple into heroic, romantic monster-fighters in a mainstream, studio film.

From the use of documentary-style onscreen text in the opening segment to the continual assertion that what the audience sees really happened, the film promotes its own reality, and encourages the audience to be afraid, since it is real. The film closes with an actual quotation from Ed Warren:

> Diabolical forces are formidable. These forces are eternal, and they exist today. The fairy tale is true. The devil exists. God exists. And for us, as people, our very destiny hinges upon which one we elect to follow. – Ed Warren

In other words, the supernatural, demonic, and diabolic forces depicted in the film are real. One of the film's recurring themes is the reality of the Warren's worldview and their fight against the demonic. "God brought us together for a reason," they keep reminding each other (and the audience). The film reinforces a conservative Catholic worldview, and asserts reality of its supernatural constructions, both divine and diabolical. Yet arguably there is more in this "true story" that is untrue than true.

This chapter considers the reality and truth behind the "true story" with a focus on four key elements. The first is the construction of "Ed and Lorraine Warren" as characters in the film versus the historic ones. A key question that needs to be answered is, who is the protagonist of the film? Is it Ed and/or Lorraine, or is it Carolyn? The second element that adds to the "reality" while not necessarily being real is the shaping influence on the film of contemporary ghost-hunting television, which Ed and especially Lorraine Warren helped shape over the last three decades. The third element is the role that religion, especially Roman Catholic theology, plays in the film. While the brothers Hayes claim they intended to write a Christian film, the Warrens belonged to a traditional sect of Catholicism that rejected the tenets of the Second Vatican Council. While the film papers over these differences, the tension between them shows again how the film uses religion to create "reality," when the actual reality is quite different. Lastly, Bathsheba Sherman is called a witch, and the film claims she was descended from the Salem witches. The film uses the horror genre conception of witches to make the antagonist seem more terrifying, but it does so at the expense of historic reality, not to mention offending a number of critics.

WHO IS THE PROTAGONIST?

One of the more interesting aspects of *The Conjuring* is that it appears to have a tripartite protagonist. Ed Warren and Lorraine Warren seem to serve as a collective protagonist, although each character also has her or his own arc and concerns. The film opens and closes with them. They appear to be the center of the film. *The Conjuring*, however, maintains the tension of a horror film by elevating Carolyn to co-protagonist – she is the one slowly becoming possessed, and Ed and Lorraine are the heroes who must overcome.

In this, the film echoes earlier horror films such as *The Exorcist*. Regan MacNeil is the possessed victim of Pazuzu, and she is the one who needs an exorcism, and much of the first half of that film focuses on her. Yet the film seems to split into two more stories – the first is that of her mother, Chris McNeill, attempting to figure out what is wrong with her daughter and get her the help (and exorcism) she needs. The film chronicles Chris's journey from concern to confusion to belief. The second is that of Father Damien Karras, whose story parallels Regan's and Chris's in the film, as he, a Jesuit psychiatrist, grapples with his own loss of faith after the death of his mother and the confrontation with the evil that is in Regan. It is only by undergoing the exorcism that Karras, Regan and Chris can complete their character arcs. *The Conjuring* follows this pattern, as the audience witnesses the fear and concern the Warrens have in that their cases have the power to greatly harm them, while simultaneously seeing Carolyn Perron slowly becoming possessed. Once again, a climactic exorcism is needed in order to restore all three characters to the state to which they belong.

The Conjuring, however, can also thus be read subversively as a critique of the Warrens – they would take other people's stories and make them about themselves. They would interject themselves into other people's crisis situations and then reap the publicity, which was the accusation against them in the Amityville case, the Snedeker case, and the Enfield poltergeist case (the basis for *The Conjuring 2*), among many others. *The Conjuring* does exactly what Ed and Lorraine Warren did: take the Perrons' family crisis and make it about Ed and Lorraine Warren.

THE WARREN FILES; OR, WILL THE REAL ED AND LORRAINE PLEASE STAND UP?

The working title of *The Conjuring* was *The Warren Files*. From its origin, the film's focus on the couple was the appeal for Wan, who said, "I really didn't want to make another haunted house or ghost story movie, but the fact that it's the Warrens is what attracted me to it. I don't see *The Conjuring* as a ghost story or a haunted house film; I see it basically as a true-life story about these two people who are very fascinating" (Snellings 2013, 30). The Warrens were to be the focus of the film, and while many horror films employ the "based on a true story" trope, no matter how loosely (*Psycho* [1960,

Alfred Hitchcock], *The Texas Chainsaw Massacre*, and *The Silence of the Lambs* [1991, Jonathan Demme] were all to some degree based on the "true story" of Ed Gein), the "true story" of *The Conjuring* was at the heart of both the marketing materials and the filmmaker's approach. In an interview on the *Annabelle: Creation* DVD, Wan says, "When I started out with *The Conjuring*, I think the true-life aspect of the story made me want to elevate it above the typical run of the mill horror film that we're kind of used to seeing. It's a drama that deals with systematic occurrences." For Wan, the horror that elevates *The Conjuring* is the fact that it is based on the "true story" of the Warrens. But is it?

The real Warrens did work as an investigatory team who were very successful at self-promotion and who also promoted a view of the world as a place of constant spiritual warfare. In their lectures, the Warrens would caution that the real problem with contemporary spirituality is not that people do not believe in God but that people do not believe in the Devil or in spiritual evil. Ed is the demonologist, Lorraine is a "sensitive," in all sense of the word (having met him, I jokingly call Ed a "working class demonologist" – Patrick Wilson captures his essence but makes him a bit too suave; watch interviews with Ed and you'll see what I mean). The Warrens have been well documented and well publicized, mostly by the Warrens themselves in a series of books, presence on television programs, etc. The dynamic in the film matches at least their public personas.

The filmmakers also went out of their way both to involve Lorraine (Ed having passed away in 2006) and to promote her involvement in the film. The "true story" was vital both for the marketing and for the scares. Lorraine Warren served as "consultant" to the film, has a cameo, and supported the making of the film. The Perron family also supported the film and visited the set. Patrick Wilson and Vera Farmiga spent time with Lorraine in her Connecticut home, preparing for the film. Farmiga reports that she was interested in capturing the nuances of how Warren's clairvoyance works:

> Patrick and I live in the tri-state area, and we visited her in Connecticut for one day. We sat down in her living room, with her roosters running around who live in the space with her, and we gathered those details…For me, in contemplating clairvoyance and how I was going to project that had to do with her eyes, in particular. She has just beautiful blue eyes that bore holes. … Her eyes are just luminous dimensional marbles

full of love and goodness, it's hard to look away… There was, for me, a bit of shyness that quickly dissipated. I can only imagine if I was 80-something and some Hollywood studio sent some punk to say they were going to represent my life, I mean I would be little suspicious, but there's none of that with her. She's just a heart on two feet and full of love. (quoted in Vancheri 2013)

The dialogue concerning Annabelle in the opening scene is taken verbatim from Gerald Brittle's The Demonologist.

While both actors were invited into the real occult museum in the Warrens' home, only Patrick Wilson went in and spent time with the allegedly cursed and haunted objects. Farmiga also reported that subsequently, on set, "odd things happened, weird things happened" (Vancheri 2013).

In other words, it was important to those involved in the film that they recreate who the Warrens "really" are and represent on the screen the alleged reality of the Perron narrative. In addition to the Perron case, the film also touches upon several other well-known and documented actual Warren cases: Annabelle the possessed doll, and Maurice, "a French-Canadian farmer with no more than a third-grade education. Yet after he was possessed, he spoke some of the best Latin I've ever heard. Sometimes backwards," as Ed (Patrick Wilson) says in the film.

Interestingly, as a result, the most accurate part of the film may be the opening. The dialogue with the nurses about Annabelle is taken almost verbatim from the transcript

Ed Warren's photo with Patrick Wilson's name in the end credits, linking the real man to the performance the audience just witnessed.

of the sessions, found in Gerald Brittle's The Demonologist, with lines like "To begin with, there is no Annabelle! There never was!" taken directly from the text (1980, 49). The opening sequence is a fairly accurate depiction of what happened, according to Brittle, ending with the Warrens taking Annabelle back to their home and placing her in a glass box (1980, 53). The facts of the Perron case, however, are not so cut-and-dry, especially since they were not detailed in any of the Warrens' books in the way that Annabelle, Maurice or the Smurl family were.

Wan also uses a number of techniques within the film to impress on the audience that what they are watching is as much documentary as narrative film, a recreation of what actually happened in Rhode Island almost fifty years ago. The end title credits make the link between the film and real life obvious by using actual newspaper accounts of the Warrens, and then by placing photos of the real people (Ed and Lorraine, the Perron family), with the names of the actors who played them in the film. For example, the first photo is of an older Ed Warren. Patrick Wilson's name, however, is the one next to the image. The implication is that the film presents these people (and by extension the situation) exactly as they were in life, further implying that the film presented what actually happened.

Yet, the real-life Warrens have faced substantial criticism, revived in the face of The Conjuring, questioning whether it was indeed "based on a true story" and whether the

Warrens were what they are depicted to be in the film or even claimed to be in real life. After the film was released a number of publications, both print and online, explored how much of *The Conjuring* was a true story. They reached a variety of conclusions.

It is obvious that *The Conjuring* takes a number of liberties with the facts. The actual Perron family lived in the farmhouse for a decade, from January 1971 until July 1980. Bathsheba Sherman (1812-1885), married Judson Sherman, as the film claims. They had at least four children, only one of whom, son Herbert, reached adulthood. He died at age 37. Bathsheba died at the age of 73 from a stroke (Bartholomew and Nickell 2015, 77). Thus, she neither killed her child right after birth, nor hanged herself. Allegedly a local infant died while in her care, and rumors spread she had killed the child herself by inserting a sewing needle (in some versions it was a knitting needle) at the base of the skull. Considering she was never arrested or tried for the crime, it is difficult to say with any certainty if it happened or not. Local folklore claims she was a witch, but there is no hard evidence that she was or was not (other than the fact that witches as depicted in popular culture simply don't exist).

Ed Warren never attempted an exorcism, as he knew they could only be performed by an ordained priest. Instead, Carolyn Perron became "temporarily possessed" during a séance (Alexander 2013). The entire climax of the film is a fictional construct. Andrea Perron herself, oldest daughter of the family and author of a three-volume series on the Perron family's experiences in the farmhouse, called the film "a beautiful tapestry" with "many elements of truth to it, and some moments of fiction" (Alexander 2013). *The Conjuring* might be "based" on a true story, but that story serves more as inspiration than beat sheet.

The Warrens themselves also come under a great deal of criticism, with allegations that their marriage was "a far cry from the one portrayed onscreen" (Masters and Cullins 2017). Joe Nickell and Robert Bartholomew assert that the film has numerous factual errors, from Roger Perron's profession (he was a travelling salesman, not a truck driver) to the idea that Carolyn sought out Ed and Lorraine Warren (Nickell and Bartholomew contend "they just showed up on a night soon before Halloween 1973") (2015, 59; 61). Carolyn was the one who interpreted events as supernatural; Roger was only told about a séance an hour before it happened, and it is alleged he subsequently tried to punch

Ed in the face, demanding the Warrens leave (Nickell and Bartholomew 2015, 71-2). Andrea Perron's books bear out this version of events.

Joe Nickell has written several articles on *The Conjuring* for *The Skeptical Inquirer*, further debunking the claims of the film (Nickell 2014; Nickell 2016). In fairness to the Warrens, however, Nickell does the same thing that he claims paranormal investigators (including the Warrens) do: take the evidence and assert that the possibility that best suits their predetermined worldview must be what happened (for example, in reporting that Andrea Perron saw an apparition in her bedroom at night, Nickells asserts, without any actual evidence or proof that Andrea was looking at her own reflection in a window [2016, 23]). Others have asserted that the Warrens have a history that could just as easily be read as hoaxes. *The Amityville Horror* is alleged to have been a hoax, but the Warrens still claimed it to be real. Horror writer Ray Garton, who worked with the Warrens on the book *In a Dark Place: The True Story of a Haunting*, claimed that the entire story behind the book was problematic at best and fraudulent at worst:

> I went to Connecticut and spent time with the Warrens and the Snedekers. When I found that the Snedekers couldn't keep their individual stories straight, I went to Ed Warren and explained the problem. "They're crazy," he said. "All the people who come to us are crazy, that's why they come to us. Just use what you can and make the rest up. You write scary books, right? Well, make it up and make it scary. That's why we hired you." (quoted in Bendici 2009).

The jury is out on whether the Warrens sincerely believed what they did and lectured upon, but what is not in doubt is that they were arguably the best known paranormal investigators in television history and created their own paranormal culture empire with books, television shows and films based on their cases, and an extensive lecture series, often at colleges and universities, for all of their career: "The Warrens didn't take fees for their work, but they enjoyed immense financial success nonetheless thanks to nine books, a busy lecture schedule and consulting on films based on their exploits" (Masters and Cullins 2017). None of this controversy is present in the film, nor, in fairness, need it be, as that is not the story Wan wants to tell. But as a result, that "true story" is perhaps a little less true than the film and filmmakers would claim.

Paranormal Investigation TV and *The Conjuring*

Several documentary-type television programs from the eighties and nineties featured occasional segments with the Warrens, from *In Search Of* (1976-1982) through *Sightings* (1991-1997) to *Unsolved Mysteries* (1987-2010). The twenty-first century, however, has seen an explosion of television shows solely dedicated to the investigation of the paranormal, especially hauntings, by amateur investigators. Sharon A. Hill argues that "The popularity of the 21st century ghost hunter can be directly linked to two television programs: *Most Haunted* in the U.K. (2002) and *Ghost Hunters* in the U.S. (2004)" (2017, 52). From these came a flood of other programs: *A Haunting* (2005-2019), *Ghost Adventures* (2008-), *Paranormal State* (2007-2011), *School Spirits* (2011-2012), *My Ghost Story* (2010-2013), *Celebrity Ghost Stories* (2008-2014), *Celebrity Ghost Stories UK* (2011), *The Haunted* (2009-2011), *The Haunted Collector* (2011-2013, featuring the Warrens' nephew John Zaffis), *Scariest Places on Earth* (2000-2006), and *Paranormal Lockdown* (2016-2019). Marc A. Eaton observes that between 2004 and 2012, "at least 31 paranormal reality television shows aired in the United States" (2015, 391). Hill refers to the groups that appear in these shows as "Amateur Research and Investigation Groups" or ARIGs (2017, 2). This designation distinguishes them from the Warrens, who billed themselves as professional "Consultants of Demonology and Witchcraft."

The rise of these groups and shows can be tied to a post-9/11 resurgence in belief in the paranormal and supernatural. Mike Hale sees in this brand of reality television "a nation's resurgent interest in things it can't see (or easily defend itself against)" (2009). I would further argue such shows demonstrate the cultural trend of the "amateur expert" – the idea that one need no formal training to develop expertise in something (and in fairness, the Warrens do not necessarily have "formal training" either). Opinion matters as much as fact or analysis in our contemporary culture, and so plumbers are just as qualified as trained experts to investigate ghosts, so long as they can afford the equipment. Lastly, I have argued elsewhere, however, that there exist multiple reasons for the explosion of ghost shows and ghost hunters after 9/11. While ghosts represent that which we cannot "defend against," ghosts also represent the idea that death is not the end, and that something of those who perish lives on after them, which has a very strong appeal after national crises in which large numbers of people have died (Wetmore 2012, 156).

Furthermore, Lorraine Warren has frequently been featured as a guest on several of these programs, including episodes of *Paranormal State*, *The Haunting*, *Is It Real?* and *Paranormal Lockdown* as well as "documentaries" such as *A Haunting in Connecticut* (2002, John Kavanagh), *American Ghost Hunter* (2010, Chad Calek), and *My Amityville Horror* (2012, Eric Walter), thus framing herself and Ed as the original celebrity paranormal investigators. *The Conjuring* is structured in a sense to echo audience expectations of television ghost hunters – a "scientific exploration" that also includes people with spiritual gifts or psychic abilities and happening in a place that is historically likely to be haunted.

Marc A. Eaton observes that, "Reality-style paranormal investigation shows also perpetuate folkloric tropes in which ghosts are more likely to haunt certain types of places" (2019, 157). Death, suicide, the murder of children, and the suffering of the mentally ill, especially if they were confined and tortured are the favorite histories of places to investigate on these programs. *The Conjuring* is set in an ideal television paranormal investigation show: a house built over a century and a half ago, in which an alleged witch killed her child and then herself, and a hundred years later another mother was thought to have killed her child, who disappeared, but the historic record is not clear. The ambiguity of the last would particularly appeal to such shows, as there is a mystery with no set answer, nor is there one really possible. The investigators are thus free to come in and construct a narrative that fits the facts as they are, but also make for great television. The house also appears old, has a scary, boarded-up cellar, and seems somewhat isolated from the neighbors, having a pond behind it and woods on either side, with only the road passing at a distance in front of the house. Such a house must be haunted, in folkloric terms.

Not only that, but the farmhouse is set in what H.P. Lovecraft frequently calls "witch-haunted New England." Rhode Island, however, is an outlier. Although the colony legislated the death penalty for witchcraft in 1647, there were no trials or executions, or even accusations. Whereas Connecticut, Maine, New Hampshire and especially Massachusetts had witch trials and executions in the seventeenth century, Rhode Island did not. By the 1660s, the colony had actually outlawed witchcraft trials. These facts, however, do not stop the folkloric belief that witch-related places in New England are by nature haunted (see: Salem).

"Give us a sign of your presence." Filming Ed and Lorraine investigating the basement echoes contemporary paranormal investigation television programs.

Eaton also observes that the places haunted in those houses tend to be the liminal ones: attics, stairways and basements are the scary places in houses (2019, 157). Of course, much of the terror in *The Conjuring* is found in the basement, although the first major incursion is on the stairway, when some force knocks down all the family photos.

As these shows depict places of real hauntings they follow the same structure: the occupant experiences inexplicable, possibly paranormal activity. They grow concerned that there may be something evil lurking in their home. They contact the paranormal investigation team who then agree to investigate. The team carries out a set of investigatory tasks, with one individual usually tasked with carrying out local and historical research, one person interviews the occupants and any other affected parties. The location is then explored and technology is then brought in to investigate to see if there is any sort of supernatural presence that can be detected: cameras, thermometers, EV meters, recording devices, etc. The possible entities are asked directly by the investigators to communicate with them. Mysterious things happen while the team is on site, some of which can be explained away, but many of which cannot.

The Conjuring follows this formula to the letter. The Perrons begin to experience strange phenomena in their home. Carolyn reaches out to paranormal investigators she has seen through popular culture (the Warrens). They visit the home and the psychic one senses an evil presence. They research the farm and learn about the history of

Bathsheba Sherman, relative of a Salem witch and a child-murdering suicide. They interview the family and the history and personal narratives reinforce one another. In other words, television ghost hunting shows and *The Conjuring* become mutually reinforcing presentations of what a "real" haunting looks like, and much of *The Conjuring*'s power comes from creating sequences that mimic ghost hunting shows but actually have something supernatural or horrific happen.

Eaton maps out a five-part narrative structure of ghost hunting shows. The first is "Narrative Priming," in which the investigators discuss the historic narratives of the site and the expectations of what happens at a haunted place, creating a hermeneutic for all of the events which follow (2019, 162). The actual investigation constitutes the second and third phases of the narrative structure. "Narrative Emergence" occurs when people experience something unexpected and overlay that with the expectations created during narrative priming (2019, 164). "Narrative Contestation" then occurs when competing interpretations and explanations are offered, although priority is given to both "higher status" individuals (such as the Warrens) and interpretations that reinforce the idea that the haunting is real (2019, 165). "Narrative Coalescence" involves the entire group of investigators comparing experiences and creating a single group narrative about "what happened" (2019, 169). The final phase is "Narrative Crystallization" in which the group narrative is confirmed as the "real" account of what happened and all other possible explanations or interpretations are excluded (2019, 172-3).

The Conjuring offers a meta version of this structure. The film itself follows it, beginning with the Annabelle sequence as a form of Narrative Priming. This is followed within the Warren narrative by a scene in which Ed and Lorraine prove that a house is not haunted and assert that what most people perceive as hauntings have mundane, non-supernatural explanations (Narrative Emergence/Narrative Contestation), while simultaneously the Perrons experience a variety of occurrences that are Narrative Emergence followed by Narrative Contestation: the smell, the clocks stopping, Christina being dragged off her bed at night, and then finally the two evenings of major occurrences: the unseen (by all but Christine) presence in Christine and Nancy's room and the following event, in which Carolyn is trapped in the basement while Bathsheba appears on top of Andrea's wardrobe and tackles her to the ground. In all these events, Roger Perron continually offers alternative explanations other than the supernatural.

THE CONJURING

There then follows the Warren's investigation of the Perrons, which begins with Narrative Priming. Ed and Lorraine learn about the history of the house – Bathsheba Sherman, a relative of one of the women hanged as a witch in Salem, and the mother who killed her child then killed herself in the basement, creating the hermeneutic for all that follows. Officer Brad and Drew, the Warrens' assistant, offer competing narratives for things that happen in the house ("It was probably a draft").

The Conjuring follows Eaton's structure for a real (read: television) paranormal investigation. In fact, in some senses, the Warrens pioneered this structure. Certainly, the narrative accounts of the Warrens in various books and television programs follow this structure. *The Conjuring* does what ghost hunting shows wish they could do: it shows the reality of a haunting in a manner that is unambiguous and definite. The challenge of paranormal investigatory television is that it cannot (or at least never has) captured definitive proof of the supernatural. Paranormal investigators reach conclusions based upon circumstantial evidence, they give interpretation of events the widest latitude – if it is remotely possible that the event is supernatural, then it must be. No other explanation need be considered. *The Conjuring* removes even the possibility of doubt, however, and does not require this interpretive space. The haunting is real, the possession is real, and the Warrens have verifiable scientific proof and video recorded evidence.

The entire cellar investigation sequence once the Warrens arrive at the Perron home reads as a television ghost hunting series. Ed tells Brad to get the camera. Cut to a shot of a light coming on and showing Brad's shoes. We are now seeing Brad's camera POV. Ed holds a microphone and wears earphones. Ed looks at his watch and says, "All right, it's 9:18, we're headed down into the cellar where the door's just opened on its own. I have Lorraine and Officer Brad Hamilton with me." This trope is taken straight out of ghost hunting shows – direct address of camera, explaining action, preparing to enter the scary place. Ed tells them to keep the cellar light off – they will only use the camera light, which continues to echo the television ghost hunting experience, where often the only light source is that provided by the investigators, usually a camera light or other small light source, the better to scare you with in the otherwise dark space. The camera captures the investigation in real time, and we are aware of both camera and the person holding it. Ed then practices electronic voice phenomenon (EVP) recording – saying,

"Give us a sign you want to communicate with us," and holding up the microphone, a trope familiar from every ghost investigation on television. We see edited shots of Ed walking around the basement, lit only by the camera light, holding the microphone out and looking behind items into dark places. He barks out orders to the spirits: "Close a door. Move something. Come on!" The camera watches, looks around. We wait. Nothing happens. We know things happen in the cellar; we have seen all the things Ed has asked for. But the spirits do not perform on command. As they head back up the stairs, Ed stops, looks around. The camera turns and looks back at the piano at the bottom of the stairs. Ed may as well ask, "Did you hear that?" – a classic ghost hunting show technique.

In short, *The Conjuring* relies on the audience's familiarity with the tropes, structures and techniques of paranormal investigation television in order to set up some of its scares. These programs have shown the audience what a "real" haunting looks like and creates expectations for how an investigation can and should be run. The script follows these structures and tropes in a quite obvious manner. *The Conjuring* seems authentic since it mimics and echoes what we have seen of documentary investigations of alleged haunted places on paranormal investigation shows. We know how to watch *The Conjuring* as *Most Haunted* and *Ghost Hunters* have already trained us how.

RELIGION AND *THE CONJURING*

In addition to relying upon the Warrens' pop culture presence and the model of paranormal investigatory television, *The Conjuring* also lives quite comfortably in the world of Christianity and contemporary religious belief. Its screenwriters see it as a Christian film, as do some of its detractors. In an article for *Vice* titled "Why Are So Many Horror Films Christian Propaganda?," Josiah M. Hesse makes clear that he sees *The Conjuring* as a proselytizing film. Quoting Hector Avalos, professor of religious studies at Iowa State University, he notes:

> Many filmmakers believe in the message of their films. They see their jobs as being missionaries for Christianity, and film is their missionary tool. Fear is a missionary tool. The message is that evil is real enough to be feared, and that you should view Christianity or religion as the best answer. (Hesse 2016)

While Wan does not see *The Conjuring* as a "missionary tool," the Warrens and the screenwriters certainly would. The film was marketed to faith groups. Advance screenings were held for them, including a showing just for priests, which makes sense – *The Conjuring* is a possession/exorcism film pretending to be a haunted house movie.

Chad and Carey Hayes, the brothers who wrote *The Conjuring* screenplay, freely admit their Christian faith was the inspiration and guiding principle behind the film: "We wanted to discuss God, faith, and the challenge to non-belief in a time of crisis" (Ryan 2013). For the brothers Hayes, the larger Truth of *The Conjuring* is more significant than the factual history of the Warrens and the Perrons.

There may be something to that theory, especially since belief in the supernatural by definition means believing in things "above nature," from ghosts to God. In the case of both of ghosts and God, faith is required for belief, and for some, faith in one implies faith in the other. They are, after all, encountered in similar ways. In his seminal volume, *The Idea of the Holy*, Rudolf Otto writes:

> Before religious dread comes 'daemonic dread' with its queer perversion, a sort of abortive offshoot, the 'dread of ghosts.' It first begins to stir in the feeling of 'something uncanny', 'eerie', or 'weird'. It is this feeling which, emerging in the mind of primeval man, forms the starting point for the entire religious development in history. (1958: 14)

Some of us may believe in a higher power because we can feel it, because we have a sense of something greater than us. We may also believe in the eerie and the haunted, as we can also feel that, and have a sense of something beyond us that is not divine, and may, in fact, be its diabolical opposite. Fear of God and fear of ghosts walk in the same continuum. Marc A. Eaton observes, "Paranormal investigation functioned as a spiritual practice for many investigators in that it allowed them to feel like they were connecting to 'a divine, supernatural, or transcendent order of reality'" (2015, 397). Ed and Lorraine Warren, both in the film and in life, present a Catholic belief structure that is underpinned by the reality of the Devil and demons.

Ed's faith in a sense is louder than Lorraine's. She carries a rosary and Vera Farmiga's performance creates a woman who carries herself with a quiet strength born of faith.

Ed's religion is worn on his sleeve and is his strongest weapon against evil. Ed places religious icons around the Perron house during the investigatory stage, telling Roger that holy objects "will get a reaction from anything unholy." The film frames the actual experience as a supernatural battle: the forces of good (the Warrens, the Church and, by extension, God), against the forces of the unholy, the demonic, and evil.

Ed's next statement, however, is that the presence of holy objects, "Sort of pisses them off," the scatological description serving to ground Ed again as a working-class demonologist with a foot very much in the real world, just as William Peter Blatty and William Friedkin did by having Father Damien Karras be a drinking, smoking, boxing, kid-from-the-old-neighborhood priest. This character construction is useful, especially in horror films. Saints are impossible things, but the holy man who also swears, drinks beer and is down to earth is a much more attainable model. From Ed Warren to Father Perez in *Annabelle* to Rafael in *The Curse of La Llorona*, the *Conjuring* universe likes its demon fighters to be holy and earthy. They want an exorcist you can go get a beer with. The interesting thing is that by grounding the opposition to the demonic in such individuals, the conflict of the film is rendered more real. Less *The Song of Bernadette* (1943, Henry King) and more *Rocky* (1976, John G. Avildsen).

Religion is also vital to the narrative because, as noted above, *The Conjuring* is really a possession film. The great irony of the film is that the hero demonologist is unable to actually dispel demons. As Ed the character states in the film, he cannot perform an exorcism. As a believing, practicing Catholic he knows he may not perform one, and doing so would be incredibly dangerous. Yet the film shows Ed agreeing to do it at the urging of Lorraine. Interestingly, the exorcism he begins to perform is from the *Rituale Romanum* (Roman Ritual), the book in which the Catholic Rite of Exorcism is found, but the one he chooses to perform is the rite to exorcize a place, not a person. The rite that cinematic audiences are familiar with is the "Western Rite of Exorcism," established in Latin in 1614 and for the purpose of freeing a possessed individual. This is the exorcism used in films such as *The Exorcist* and its sequels, *The Rite*, and many, many others.

The ritual Ed begins to recite in *The Conjuring*, however, is the "Exorcism against Satan and His Fallen Angels for a Particular Geographic Place," and is designed to exorcise a

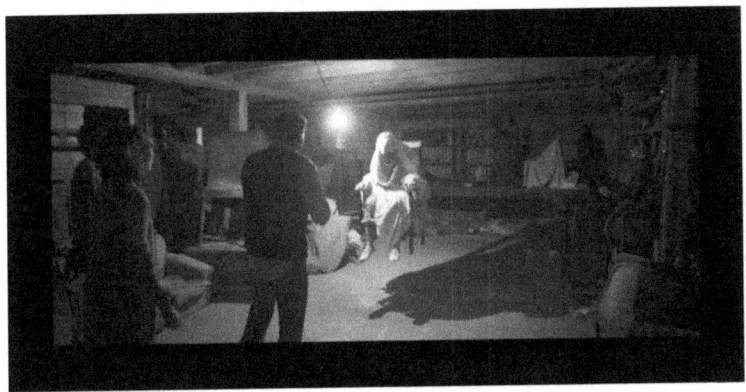

The exorcism in the basement.

specific location, not a person. It begins with the prayer to St. Michael the Archangel, which is what Ed recites in Latin during the exorcism of Carolyn Perron. This rite is much shorter than the one for people, consisting of the prayer to St. Michael, the prayer of exorcism, Psalm 67, the second prayer of exorcism, and then ends with sprinkling the locality with holy water (see Burton 2017).

The question must then be asked, why the ritual to exorcize a place instead of a person for Carolyn Perron? The film contains several possibilities. Ed might be employing the easier, shorter ritual out of efficiency. Ed, knowing he is doing something the Church forbids, decides to go for the lesser ritual so that it is less of a sin. Ed knows he is not permitted to carry out the ritual to exorcise people, as he is not a priest. He technically cannot perform the one for places either, which can only be done by bishops or priests with the bishop's approval (Burton 2017, 68). The film shows the character of Ed deciding that his performing the exorcism of place is less of a sin, as the exorcism of people invokes the priest's authority on behalf of the church and Christ, whereas the locale rite is entirely about God doing it. Hence the former features lines (again, familiar from *The Exorcist*) such as "I cast you out," "I command you," and "I who, though unworthy, am a minister of God" – centering the clash of the exorcism between the demonic and the exorcist who operates for and in the name of the Church, whereas the latter contains no "I statements," but only "we statements," such as "we cast thee out," or invokes God directly, rather than claiming to act on God's behalf (Burton 2017,

25; 70). The exorcism of a place is not a personal conflict but a group effort. It might also be that Ed knows getting Bathsheba out of Carolyn does not get rid of Bathsheba, but the locale exorcism gets her out of the house as well as the woman she has possessed. Lastly, the prayer to St. Michael the Archangel in Latin sounds really cool and uses all the cool exorcism words. The ritual for a person begins with the Litany of the Saints, and even if you skip that (which, for example, *The Exorcist* does), the next moments are the "Our Father," followed by Psalm 53, and a call and response prayer. Not nearly as dynamic and interesting as the Latin prayer from the ritual Ed uses.

All of this is because there is a conflicted Catholicism hidden within *The Conjuring*. In 1962, Pope John XXIII called for the Second Vatican Council (AKA Vatican II), announcing in *Gaudet Mater Ecclesia* ("Mother Church Rejoices") that the Church's teachings are eternal, but, "What is needed is that this certain and immutable doctrine, to which the faithful owe obedience, be studied afresh and reformulated in contemporary terms" (1962). In other words, John XXIII intended to bring the Church into the twentieth century. Numerous conservative Catholics resisted this call. Pre-Vatican II Catholicism is essentially medieval, anti-modernist Catholicism. *The Conjuring* is set in 1971, just six years after the end of the Second Vatican Council. All of the reforms and changes were both new and ongoing. Traditional Catholics and those who preferred the older ways believed the Church had lost its foundation in order to be "relevant" in the sixties. The Warrens are conservative Catholics who prefer the older, Latin mass, and who seem to reject the new theologies emerging out of the Second Vatican Council, which, it should be noted, focused a great deal less on Satan and evil and much more on a loving God in Christ.

The film wears its traditional Catholicism on its sleeve. As a result, the film is problematized by the fact that Ed Warren would never be sanctioned to carry out an exorcism. A 29 September 1985 letter from Cardinal Joseph Ratzinger, the future Pope Benedict XVI, then Prefect for the Congregation of the Doctrine of the Faith, to all Roman Catholic bishops began: "Recent years have seen an increase in the number of prayer groups in the Church aimed at seeking deliverance from the influence of demons, while not actually engaging in real exorcisms. These meetings are led by lay people, even when a priest is present" (Ratzinger 1985).

Canon 1172 of the Code of Canon Law states that only priests may perform exorcisms and only with the permission of the local bishops. In the same letter from Cardinal Ratzinger, he makes clear that Catholics are forbidden to do exactly what Ed Warren does in this film: "those who are without the due faculty may not conduct meetings during which invocations, to obtain release, are uttered in which demons are questioned directly and their identity sought to be known."

The films in *The Conjuring* franchise are shaped by the Second Vatican Council through their association with the Warrens. Ed and Lorraine Warren claimed to be the only lay people sanctioned by the Catholic Church to fight demons, and Ed claimed to be "the only Catholic lay demonologist." There are no records in the Church or produced by the Warrens to support these claims, but their Catholicism is on display, both in their public personas and as constructed by *The Conjuring*. The reality may be a little more complex.

Traditionalist Catholics strongly objected to the reforms of the Second Vatican Council, with many Catholics refusing to adopt them, preferring the Tridentine Mass, also known as the Traditional Latin Mass: the prayers and services used by the Church until 1962. Ed and Lorraine Warren seem to have been Tridentine Catholics, and certainly the presentation of them in *The Conjuring* bears up on this. Ed prays in Latin and uses the traditional prayer to St. Michael the Archangel in Latin to begin his "exorcism" of Carolyn. As seen in *The Exorcist* (released two years after *The Conjuring* is set), the Roman Ritual, the prayer book in which the Rite of Exorcism is found, is in English after Vatican II.

Father Gordon in the *Conjuring* films was based upon Bishop Robert McKenna, O.P. (1927-2015), a longtime associate of the Warrens and Tridentine Catholic who believed in sedeprivationism; that is to say that he only performed mass in Latin, did not accept the reforms of Vatican II, and believed all popes after Paul VI were illegitimate. He was an exorcist who worked with the Warrens, among others, preaching the reality of the Devil, but he had been consecrated a bishop in 1986 without Papal mandate, and was subsequently excommunicated from the Roman Catholic Church. All of this seems to suggest that the Warrens' own connection to the institutional church is indirect at best. Which means in a film "based on a true story," the God that brought Ed and Lorraine Warren together for a reason is one about whom they carry unresolved issues in regard to His one, holy, Catholic, apostolic (or maybe not) Church.

Even if disputes, theological or otherwise, within Catholicism are irrelevant to the film, its religion is both part of the "true story" aspect and part of its effectiveness at causing anxiety and fear. Douglas E. Cowan observes both an antipathy towards religion in horror cinema (including its power to motivate horror and its powerlessness in the face of actual horror), and towards horror among religious critics, observing one reviewer calling horror second only to pornography in offending religious sensibilities (2008, 43). And yet, films such as *The Exorcist*, *The Omen* and *Rosemary's Baby* (1968, Roman Polanski) (and thus, *The Conjuring*) generate a different kind of fear for the believing audience member, as the horror is not merely metaphoric, or can be understood through psychoanalysis, but rather because they depict a reality that is terrifying. For the viewer who believes, the Devil is real, the demonic is real. Both the Warrens and the brothers Hayes would state that the horror of *The Conjuring* lies in its depiction of something that is both true and real, regardless of what the Warrens themselves sincerely believed or what church they embraced.

A WORD ON WITCHES

Andrew O'Hehir cannily observes that *The Conjuring* is "a movie about America's obsession with evil and how easily that gets pointed in the wrong direction" (2013). The perfect example of this is the Salem witches: a community in fear due to cultural and social shifts, Native American attacks, an unstable basis for the colony (since the royal charter was revoked), and a population deeply suspicious of each other for religious, ethnic and class reasons genuinely saw themselves as a God-created community under assault by Satan without and within by Satan's agents within that community – witches. Obviously, none of the people accused and/or executed in Salem were actual witches. But in American popular culture, that fact is irrelevant. Salem is now "Witch City," and witches were the first victims of what we now call a "witch hunt."

The Conjuring has received criticism in some quarters for its depiction of witches, valorization of the conservative Catholic view of the Warrens, and its medieval approach to good-versus-evil. In the film, while researching the house, Lorraine discovers that the original occupant was Bathsheba Sherman (née Thayer), a relative of Mary Towne Estye, who was executed for witchcraft in Salem. That part of the story – both Sherman's relationship with Estye and Estye's execution – is true. The question is begged by the film, though, what does the fact that Bathsheba is related to Mary Esty have to do with the haunting of the Perrons' house?

The Salem witches were most certainly not actual witches but victims of social forces and malevolent neighbors – there was no actual witchcraft in Salem and Mary Towne Estye was certainly not a real witch (for a thorough accounting of Estye and the trials, see Schiff, 2015). Brian Collins, writing in *Religious Studies Review*, observes, correctly, that: "The film operates on the assumption that witches are Satan-worshipping evildoers, not misunderstood outsiders" or even truly innocents (as not all the victims in Salem were even "misunderstood outsiders") (2013, 253-4). *The Conjuring* relies on a pop cultural, rather than historical, understanding of the Salem witches and of witchcraft in general. For progressives, the alignment of the Warrens with the witch hunters and judges of Salem is a source of horror in the film.

On one hand, then, *The Conjuring* misrepresents witchcraft and Salem, relying upon popular conceptions of both. On the other, the film benefits from and is a part of a witch renaissance occurring in the second decade of the twenty-first century – see *Season of the Witch* (2011, Dominic Sena), *Hansel & Gretel: Witch Hunters* (2013, Tommy Wirkola), *Witching & Bitching* (2013, Álex de la Iglesia), *Into the Woods* (2014, Rob Marshall), Robert Eggers' justly-celebrated *The Witch* (2015), *Blair Witch* (2016, Adam Wingard), *The Love Witch* (2016, Anna Biller), another film made in the 2010s but set in the early seventies, the remake of Argento's *Suspiria* (2018, Luca Guadagnino), television series such as *American Horror Story: Coven* (2013–14), *The Good Witch* (2015-present), and the reboot of *Charmed* (2018–) as well as *The Chilling Adventures of Sabrina* (2018–) and *Marianne* (2019) on Netflix. Witches have risen to become a dominant supernatural force in horror media and that media seems to suggest that they are powerful, dangerous, and have efficacy to work malevolence in the real world.

Virtually all of these narratives have two aspects in common. First, they all accept the reality that witches are real, are predominantly evil, and interact on some level with the Devil, in direct opposition to historic reality. Second, at heart they are all also narratives about female empowerment and male resistance to that empowerment. Witches are powerful and generally depicted as independent, which makes them a threat to patriarchal Christianity. *The Conjuring* fits well within this dynamic; its witch is evil, supernaturally endowed, and in league with the Devil. She seeks to empower mothers to kill their children, thus destroying the family unit, while also very obviously having a number of powers that can only be challenged by males, especially fathers. It is no coincidence that fighting Bathsheba is carried out initially by Ed Warren and then by a different "father" – a Catholic priest that blesses Annabelle monthly to keep her power contained, just like the "Fathers" in *The Exorcist*, who are brought in to control an adolescent woman.

We might perhaps observe that the connection to the Salem witches also returns us to the idea of seeing and not seeing discussed in chapter one. Cotton Mather (1663-1728), the Boston-based Puritan minister who was involved in the Salem witchcraft trials, encouraged the admission of "spectral evidence," the appearance of the accused in dreams and visions of the alleged victims, but warned against its overuse: "do not lay more stress on pure spectral evidence than it will bear … It is very certain that the Devils have sometimes represented the Shapes of persons not only innocent, but also very virtuous" (Mather 1971, 35; 40). In other words, one cannot always trust what one sees with witches. Mather's own account of the Salem trials is found in his book *The Wonders of the Invisible World*, by its very title purporting the dangers that cannot be seen and seeing the witches as part of "the plot of the Devil against New England" (Mather 1862, 4). He speaks of "invisible hands" that torment the girls before and during the witch trials, evidence that the torments were demonic in origin (Mather 1862, 14-15; 121). Indeed, the horror that Mather sees unfolding in New England in 1692 is that of the invisible becoming visible. That which cannot be seen takes a physical form – the Devil in the form of a horse, or a dog, or your neighbor. The Devil attacks humankind "as if the Invisible World were becoming Incarnate, on purpose for the vexing of us" (Mather 1862, 80). In other words, the invisible world becomes visible by incarnating (taking on the flesh).

Bathsheba Sherman, at least in the world of *The Conjuring*, is able to use her Devil-derived powers to be either invisible or visible in order to terrify the Perrons. She infests the house when they move in, and quickly moves to oppress the family, in the demonic sense, before finally possessing Carolyn. As Mather argues, "Which trick of rendring [sic] themselves Invisible, our Witches do in their confessions pretend that they sometimes are Masters of; and it is the more credible, because there is Demonstration that they often render many other things utterly Invisible" (Mather 1862, 128). Bathsheba becomes invisible but may still work malevolent acts in the world. This aspect makes her very dangerous, far more than a simple ghost. In other words, the danger of witches is that their evil is, for the most part, invisible, and cannot be seen by the human eye. We may not trust what we see and the damage, when we finally realize it has been done, cannot be reversed, as it is too late.

Thus *The Conjuring* creates a world in which Bathsheba Sherman is exactly what the Puritans who ran the Salem witch trials thought witches were: malevolent women (and occasionally men) who had malignant powers they could use against their neighbors, and against God's kingdom in the New World, given to them by the Devil. Let us not forget that Salem is only the most famous of the New England witchcraft trials – there were also many others over the seventeenth and early eighteenth century in Massachusetts, Maine and Connecticut, the last being one of the two states in which *The Conjuring* is set. The film codes witches as actually having genuine supernatural powers as a result of trafficking with the Devil. While the film is completely, historically wrong about Mary Towne Estye and the reality of Salem – there were no witches in Salem, and the witches as the Puritans imagined them never existed – it imagines a world in which the witch hunters of Salem were right, and that the Warrens, for all practical purposes, are their heirs, serving the same function in New England three hundred years later.

A RETURN TO THE WARRENS

Vera Farmiga, who plays Lorraine, reported a supernatural event related to the film. Interviewed by the *Pittsburgh Post-Gazette*, she related, "I had, for several hours, been researching Lorraine and watching YouTube videos, and I closed my computer screen, and I spoke with James [Wan, the director]. ... We hung up, I opened my laptop and there were these digital claw marks, and the film experience began with that" (Vancheri 2013). She subsequently reported that when she flew home the day after filming, she woke up with a bruise and three slash marks on her thigh. Farmiga claims that working on the film resulted in her having supernatural experiences, all of which also adds to the "based on a true story" mythos. Not only were the Warrens in an adversarial relationship with supernatural forces, but the actors appearing in a film about them equally fell into the same conflict with similar assaults on their person. In other words, "it's all true!"

We must conclude by reminding ourselves the Ed and Lorraine Warren ("ghost hunters, paranormal researchers, kooks, wackos," as they playfully identify themselves in the first few minutes of the film) in *The Conjuring* are only "based on" the historic Ed and Lorraine Warren and should not be conflated with them. They are fictional versions of the actual people. Wan claimed the Warrens were the reason he was drawn to the script, but it was the Warrens of the script perhaps, more than the actual Warrens. Or at least part of his interest is in the Warrens as potential "kooks." The *New York Times* review of the film praises James Wan for "smartly [keeping] enough distance from the Warrens that you can see that these true believers are also hovering at the edge of a dangerous fanaticism" (Dargis 2013). That is a fair assessment. Perhaps which version of the Warrens one sees when looking at *The Conjuring* depends on one's knowledge of and thoughts about them in real life. But "the Warrens" of *The Conjuring* are as much "based on a true story" as *The Conjuring* is.

As will be explored in greater depth in chapter four, the *Conjuring* universe, as it is known, is a mixture of narratives "based on a true story" in the Warren files and stories that are complete fictions invented by the screenwriters. *The Conjuring*, *The Conjuring 2*, and *Annabelle Comes Home* are all allegedly rooted in historic reality, whereas *Annabelle*, *Annabelle: Creation*, *The Nun* and *The Curse of La Llorona* are all completely fictitious, which means that the *Conjuring* universe is less "based on a true story" than inspired by a few alleged events and historic individuals that serve as inspiration for a series of flights of fancy.

The horror of *The Conjuring* is in part created by the idea that it is a "true story" and that such things can and do really happen. Yet, as this chapter has analyzed, much of *The Conjuring* is, technically speaking, not true. So why is it still scary? First, despite the allegations and evidence of a lack of reality undergirding the film, the marking campaign that branded the film as based on a true story was remarkably effective at keeping that designation believable. Despite critics asserting otherwise, *The Conjuring* appears on numerous "movies based on true stories" lists on the internet. In addition, the viewing experience may be rooted in the idea of the willing suspension of disbelief. Lastly, as I hope this chapter has shown, the cultural markers of paranormal investigation television, the use of religion in horror films and the coding of witches as supernatural evil ensure that the film is read by audiences as genuinely scary as it is rooted in historic "reality", even when it is not.

Chapter Three: Child's Play and Women's Work

For much of the first half of the twentieth century, horror cinema focused on the child as victim and a sentimental, almost melodramatic depiction of childhood and family. The example par excellence, of course, is the little girl in *Frankenstein* (1931, James Whale). Children were to be protected from horror, and some of the most frightening moments in early horror cinema comes from the threatening and killing of children, including and up to the "Christmas Party" sequence of *Dead of Night* (1945, Alberto Cavalcanti).

In post-war cinema, children became as threatening as threatened in such films as *The Bad Seed* (1956, Mervyn LeRoy), *Village of the Damned* (1960, Wolf Rilla) and *Lord of the Flies* (1963, Peter Brook). This trend continued and amplified through the seventies in such films as *The Other* (1972, Robert Mulligan), *It's Alive* (1974, Larry Cohen), *Alice, Sweet Alice* (1976, Alfred Sole), and *The Brood* (1979, David Cronenberg) as well as *The Omen* and its sequels. As a result, up to the present moment in cinema, children have functioned often as miniature adults – threatened and threatening, dangerous and in danger. Audiences are horrified by a child being harmed and by a child causing harm. Innocence exists side-by-side with menace and is sometimes even completely replaced by it.

There are a number of children in *The Conjuring*, from Judy Warren, Ed and Lorraine's daughter, to the five Perron sisters, to the ghostly Rory, killed by his own mother. While none of them are dangerous or horrific children, it is through their fun and games, their unintentionally dangerous curiosity (think Judy Warren in the occult museum when Ed explains how dangerous the items in the room are and she just wants to see and possibly touch them), and how easily they can be deceived that allows the children to function as a conduit for the evil in the houses (both the Warrens' and the Perrons').

"Children's culture is a minefield in the horror film," proclaims Dominic Lennard (2014, 131). Just like the Ouija board in *The Exorcist*, the game Hide-and-Clap and Rory's toy music box in *The Conjuring* serve as conduits linking the everyday world with the supernatural in *The Conjuring*. Much of the film is rooted in toys, games, and parents playing with children. Horror and childhood are inextricably interlinked, both the fear that children feel in a world that can seem scary, but also fear for children – parents and adults unable to help a child in peril (see: *The Exorcist*, *Poltergeist*, *Mama* [2013, Andy Muschietti], *Hereditary* [2018, Ari Aster], etc.), and even the fear of children (see: *The Omen*, *The Bad Seed*, *Village of the Damned*, etc.).

Toys, in particular, can become especially threatening. Likewise, games, which can seem fun and harmless, can also be activities that lead to peril, whether through their ritualistic nature, their competitive nature, or their aggressive nature (see: *Ready or Not* [2019, Matt Bettinelli-Olpin, Tyler Gillett], *Beyond the Gates* [2016, Jackson Stewart], etc.). Even adult games can result in terror, as seen in *Hellraiser* (1987, Clive Barker), where solving a puzzle box results in the opening of a gate to the dimension of the Cenobites, a kind of "hell," and great pain for everyone involved, and more recently in *Escape Room* (2019, Adam Robitel), where a popular adult group activity becomes a kill zone. If horror is a cautionary tale, one if its primary lessons is to be wary of toys and games.

Child's Play as Horror in *The Conjuring*

Game playing is important in childhood, and the idea of play comes up frequently in *The Conjuring*. The film's opening shot is a close up of a doll's face. The first line of the film is heard in the darkness of a black screen: "It scares us just thinking about it. When you hear it, you're going to think we're insane," says student nurse Debbie. Ed responds, "Try us. Please, from the start." After the voiceover there is an immediate cut to close up of the upper left side of Annabelle's face from left nostril up to her bangs: the broken blue eye, with a diamond-shaped crack in it. The rosy cheeks, also cracked, now looking like an injury with blood pooling up around it. It is an incomplete image – a fragment of a broken doll whose proximity to the camera, fractured features and hint of malevolence in the damaged eye is clearly meant to set the viewer into a state of unease. It is easy to forget after three films about the doll that this is the first thing we see in *The Conjuring* and the first time we see Annabelle, the fragment of her face that is visible suggesting that somehow the doll is incomplete – we are not seeing all of it. The nurses do not see all of it. The unbelievers do not see all of it. Only the Warrens perceive the complete truth of the doll and thus see the whole of what Annabelle truly is.

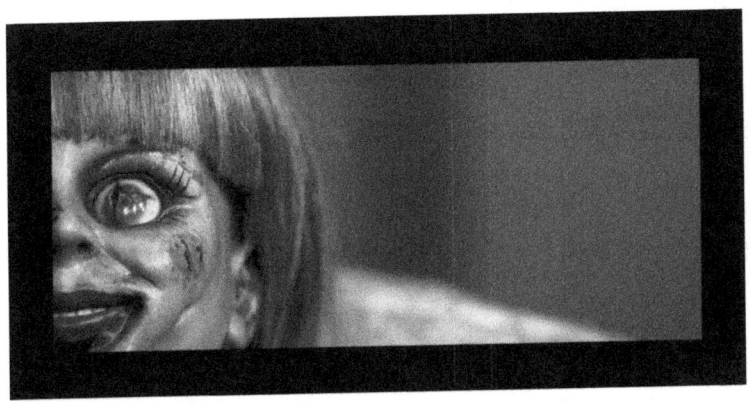

The film opens with the image of the terrifying doll Annabelle, revealed to be the conduit of a demon.

The camera begins to gradually pull back, slowly revealing the fullness of Annabelle's face. The nurses slowly tell the story of Annabelle and how she became such a frightening presence in their lives. There is something evil about Annabelle. That, the movie seems to say, should be your focus. Not the victims, but the entity.

By opening the film with the startling image of Annabelle's damaged face, Wan immediately ties the film to its predecessors concerning evil or possessed dolls or sinister animated toys, including but not limited to: *The Devil-Doll* (1936, Tod Browning), *Curse of the Doll People* (Muñecos infernales, 1961, Benito Alazraki), *Devil Doll* (1964, Lindsay Shonteff) the Zuni fetish doll sequence from *Trilogy of Terror* (1975, Dan Curtis), *The Pit* (1981, Lew Lehman), *Poltergeist*, *Dolls* (1987, Stuart Gordon), *Silent Night, Deadly Night 5: The Toy Maker* (1991, Martin Kitrosser), *Dolly Dearest* (1991, Maria Lease), *Demonic Toys* (1992, Peter Manoogian), *Pinocchio's Revenge* (1996, Kevin S. Tenney), *Small Soldiers* (1998, Joe Dante), *Doll Graveyard* (2005, Charles Band), not to mention *Child's Play* (1988, Tom Holland), *Puppet Master* (1989, David Schmoeller) and their many sequels. Michael Redgrave plays an unbalanced ventriloquist who believes his dummy is alive in one of the segments in *Dead of Night*; *Magic* (1978, Richard Attenborough) sees Anthony Hopkins' ventriloquist threatened by his own dummy, Fats; *Toy Story 4* (2019, Josh Cooley), itself part of a series that posits toys are sentient and active when humans are not around, features a group of sinister ventriloquist dummies in the service of Gabby Gaby. James Wan, of course, himself directed a killer-ventriloquist dummy film in *Dead Silence*. All of these echo the famous 1963 *Twilight Zone* episode "Living Doll," in which a mother named Annabelle(!) gives her daughter Christie a "Talking Tina" doll. The doll, which says, "My name is Talky Tina, and I love you very much," begins threatening the stepfather of the family: "My name is Talky Tina, and you'll be sorry," and "My name is Talky Tina, and I think I could even hate you," and finally, "My name is Talky Tina, and I am going to kill you" – and she does, murdering the stepfather, making it seem like an accident. She then tells the mother, "My name is Talky Tina and you better be nice to me."

Unlike these other dolls, however, Annabelle is neither a sentient doll nor the manifestation of a ventriloquist's id. The doll simply is, according to Ed, a conduit: "A very powerful demonic has latched itself onto her." The young nurses at the start of the film take pity on what they believe is the ghost of a dead child in their apartment, but which is actually "a demon that has never walked the earth in human form." This opening sequence sets up a recurring theme in the film – the dangers of toys, games, and children, or at least things masquerading as children. The entire opening sequence of *The Conjuring* is spent establishing how dangerous a doll is, and how an evil supernatural entity uses it to lure sympathetic if naïve people to open their home, lives and eventually souls to it. The danger, the film says, comes from things that seem least dangerous.

The next sequence features Ed giving a tour of the Warren's occult museum to a reporter (Arnell Powell). The toy monkey is singled out, and its nature as a toy is specified: Ed tells the reporter, "Nothing's a toy. Not even the toy monkey." What the reporter really wants to see, however, is Annabelle. She is the star of the occult museum. More than the armor, more than the television or the other various pieces of bric-a-brac in the room, it is the doll behind glass that terrifies.

Meanwhile, back at the Perron home, April, the youngest Perron daughter, discovers a toy music box that puts her in touch with "Rory," a sad child ghost that is revealed to be a real child's ghost. Rory, the audience is told, was killed by his mother while she was possessed by Bathsheba. The music box is in the shape of a circus tent. It has painted side panels showing circus scenes. When the top is lifted, inside the top is a mirrored spiraling disk. In the base is a clown head that rises and falls inside the box as the disk spins. The overall effect is a little unsettling, especially with the music. The music, in fact, will become a recurring sound motif in the film, suggesting the presence of the supernatural. The box itself, with its spiraling mirror, creepy clown head, and music box tune reads less like a children's toy and more like nightmare fuel.

Rory and his mirrored music box form a unique parallel with the doll and the demonic spirit pretending to be "Annabelle." Both supernatural entities use a toy as a conduit to connect with the living. Both entities seek connection with the living. "Annabelle," however, seeks to possess the adults who give it shelter, Rory seeks only comfort and companionship, while warning against the other entities in the house. Between the doll and the music box, however, it is clear that in the world of The Conjuring, toys are conduits by which supernatural beings can interact with and have efficacy in our reality.

April complains to Carolyn that the other children won't play with her. Andrea is too old to play and April is too young for the others to want to play with her. Cindy, Christine and Nancy form a play group, so to speak, that is exclusionary of their youngest sibling. Indeed, the film parallels the loneliness of April and Judy Warren, both of whom are threatened by Bathsheba, and both of whom are opened up to demonic toys because of an absence of other playmates for them. If one's siblings or peers won't play with one, or if one has no siblings, then one either makes them up, seeks them out, or plays in one's parents' occult museum. In the absence of other playmates, April plays with Rory. When they return from getting ice cream, April asks if the other kids want to play a game. They decline and do not want to play with her. The chief game of the middle Perron children is Hide-and-Clap, as discussed in chapter one, which becomes another means by which the spirits in the house are made manifest, with hands coming out of a wardrobe to clap when Carolyn is playing alone with April, and again when the mother is at the top of the basement stairs.

This film represents an inversion of The Exorcist, of sorts, in which playing with a Ouija board allows a child to become possessed and threaten its mother. In The Conjuring, toys and games help a mother become possessed to threaten her children. The result is a film that explores motherhood through possession and childhood through sinister toys and games. We might also note Wan's theme of sight and blindness, as discussed in chapter one – the dominant game in the film, Hide-and-Clap, requires one to be blindfolded. What is and is not seen, what one can and cannot see, what one is unwilling

Rory's music box ends up in the occult museum with Annabelle, despite having nothing to do with Bathsheba Sherman.

to see and what one is blind to, and when one willingly gives up sight in order to "play" all constitute a major theme of the film.

Game playing is prevalent in horror films, from the Ouija board in *The Exorcist* to the eponymous game in *The Black Waters of Echo's Pond* (2009, Gabriel Bologna). *Scream* features a killer who calls and asks, "Want to play a game?" Similarly, *Saw*, also directed by Wan, is a game-playing film. Jigsaw's recording to Amanda begins, "Hello Amanda. You don't know me, but I know you. I want to play a game. Here's what happens if you lose." Jigsaw focuses on the structure of game playing. He tells Zep Hindle, "There are rules." His instructions to Dr. Gordon close with, "Let the game begin," and the final line of *Saw* is: "Game over." The repeated line through the rest of the series is, "I want to play a game."

Horror films often employ Hide-and-Seek as a sinister game with larger implications as seen in such films as *Pet Sematary* (1989, Mary Lambert) and *The Good Son* (1993, Joseph Ruben), according to Lennard (2014, 131). Hide-and-Seek involves two larger elements that can seem to overlap with both paranormal investigation and horror movies. First, the game involves hiding from "it", the player designated as the one who will seek. Slasher films follow this motif – the majority of characters hide from "it," the one who seeks and who seeks to harm. Second, conversely, the game involves looking for hidden people – those who simultaneously want to be found and do not want to be found. The entity in the Perron house initially plays Hide-and-Seek with both the Perrons and the Warrens, until her true identity is uncovered. In one sense, all horror movies are Hide-and-Seek, if not cat-and-mouse.

As April's complaint shows, game playing can be exclusionary or inclusionary. One individual might be targeted in a game, or one individual might determine the fate of the other players. Every game has rules, rewards and punishments. Games reward competition and aggression and have winners and losers. Games also contain a ritual element, from counting and announcing "ready or not, here I come," to the specific practices of chess, to all of the epiphenomena that surround games of baseball and football. The game that the Warrens play has rules, rewards and punishments. There are consequences of play, as Lorraine learns with Maurice's exorcism. There are winners and losers. Game play becomes a metaphor for competition and survival within the world of *The Conjuring*.

Toys remain prevalent throughout the film, and eventually they serve to help solve the mystery of the Perron house. The uncanny music box discussed above serves as the key to understand Bathsheba's plan. While trying to remove the family from the home as Carolyn grows more possessed, Cindy vanishes in Andrea's room. Tracking her through a secret compartment in the walls, the Warrens are able to find a hidden door that leads to a secret room, which contains dust-covered shelves of old toys, including blocks, a wooden car, a top, and a music box-shaped clear space in the dust. Lorraine asks for the music box and finds it fits perfectly, identifying the space as Rory's safe room, both in life and death. They are thus able to identify Rory through his toys.

Interestingly, at the end of the film, it is not something of Bathsheba's that the Warrens place in their occult museum but the music box in which one can view Rory. He becomes the entity that is the genie kept in the bottle at the end, not the dangerous witch, not least because of this idea that toys are dangerous. Bathsheba is gone, exorcized. Rory still uses the music box as a conduit and thus must be kept in the same room as Annabelle, another toy-as-conduit. Annabelle is the queen of the occult object room, and Rory's box, as another toy, serves better than any possession of Bathsheba's. The final image of the film is the music box on the shelf, the mirror spiraling and the tune playing, suggesting Rory is now present in the room as well.

This sense of the dangerousness of childhood play continues through the series. Annabelle is featured in three films as the eponymous villain: *Annabelle*, *Annabelle: Creation*, and *Annabelle Comes Home*. She is the gift that keeps giving. Only in *Annabelle: Creation* do we see the entity using the doll. Otherwise, it is the doll itself that remains a sinister presence in the *Conjuring* Universe. The doll is a gift to an expectant mother in *Annabelle*, but it seemingly becomes possessed by a homicidal, dead cult member. *Annabelle: Creation* begins with Samuel Mullins, toymaker, creating Annabelle. The audience eventually learns that the Mullins did the exact same thing the student nurses in *The Conjuring* did: after the death of their daughter Annabelle "Bee" Mullins, he and his wife began to see signs of a haunting. On the assumption that it was actually the spirit of their daughter, they invited it to enter and take possession of Annabelle the doll, made in her memory and named after her. Instead, an evil entity occupied the doll and almost killed Mrs. Mullins multiple times through the years, before finally succeeding toward the end of the film. Mr. Mullins is also killed by the demon inside the doll.

Annabelle's old room is full of toys, many of which it is safe to assume her father made for her: a lifelike doll house, a pop gun that allows one to reel the projectile back to the gun, and other fun toys, left untouched by the orphaned girls now in the house until Janice and then Linda begin sneaking into the forbidden bedroom to play with them. It is in the forbidden bedroom, of course, that they discover the doll and unleash the spirit that uses it, leading to the many deaths.

Games are equally dangerous in the *Conjuring* Universe. The orphan girls play Hide-and-Seek in *Annabelle: Creation*, finding in it a means to childhood cruelty. When Linda, who has already abandoned her sister Janice to play with the older, more able-bodied girls, says she does not want to talk about boys with the older girls, Carol responds, "Let's play Hide-and-Seek. You go hide, and we'll come look for you." Linda runs off. Kate asks, "So are we going to look for her?" Carol smiles cruelly and responds, "Maybe." Linda hides in a secret crawlspace under the stairs, juxtaposed with the older girls exploring the barn, being startled by a scarecrow, and most decidedly not looking for Linda. Linda is startled when Annabelle is in the crawlspace below the stairs and she falls backwards out of it, only to be confronted by the older girls returning from the barn. "Found you," Carol says casually. "You're not very good at hiding." The game of Hide-and-Seek is an occasion to be exclusionary and cruel, as noted above, but it is also an occasion for Linda, while hiding, to encounter Annabelle and the demon using her, and thereby becoming alert to the danger that actually lurks in the house. Linda, while attempting to hide in play, found something rather serious and dangerous.

The Conjuring 2 features another music box-like device with "The Crooked Man," a zoetrope that summons the demon Valak in the form of the Crooked Man. Billy Hodgson in that film has a teepee set up on the upstairs landing of his family's townhouse, and its dark interior serves as a place from which darkness can emerge. A toy fire engine emerges, lights flashing and siren sounding in order to frighten the children. Later on, the zoetrope and accompanying recorded song unleashes the Crooked Man. At the end of the film, Ed brings the zoetrope back to the occult museum in the Warren home and noticeably places it next to the music box from the first film, visually linking the two. In both cases, a child's mechanical toy is revealed to be a spirit-summoning device, or at least a tool used by an entity to terrify people.

In the most recent addition to the series (as of this writing), *Annabelle Comes Home*, the theme of toys and games being a gateway into the supernatural is repeatedly literalized. In addition to the eponymous doll, Judy Warren and her babysitter, Mary Ellen, and her friend Daniela play the *Feeley Meeley* game in which players draw a card and then reach into a covered box, attempting to pull out an object matching the picture on the card. *Feeley Meeley* was, in fact, a real game created by Milton Bradley in 1967. It came with twenty-four small objects and matching cards. The game is an exercise in touching that which you cannot see, with an added anxiety factor, suggestive of the old Halloween game of placing one's hand in a bowl to touch a zombie's brains, eyes, fingers and other body parts. It relies on tactile experience without vision, which can also induce anxiety. The film presents the box as not just containing terrifying objects, but also capable of grabbing players and pulling them into the box. *Feeley Meeley* becomes simply another Lament Configuration, opening the gates of hell for anyone who plays.

Later in the film, when Annabelle locks herself in a closet as the spirits of the occult museum roam free, a card from the game slides out from under the door depicting a key. Mary Ellen must reach into the *Feeley Meeley* game box to find it. As she reaches, Judy slams her hand into the other side and immediately pulls out the key, unlocking the closet door and discovering a room full of corpses standing upright in caskets, all with coins over their eyes instead of the closet. As Mary Ellen approaches the last corpse, she sees it is hers. Her own dead body stands upright with coins over the eyes, and it is holding Annabelle. The game leads to another seeming game which leads to the doll. When Daniela, possessed by the wedding dress, attacks Mary Ellen, hands come out of the *Feeley Meeley* box to grasp at and restrain Judy.

Of significance is the fact that Mary Ellen, Daniela and Judy select *Feeley Meeley* from a stack of board games that includes *Let's Make a Deal*, *Battleship*, *Life*, *Monopoly*, *Password*, *Sorry*, *Booby-Trap*, and several more. What all of these toys and games do is to take the familiar and de-familiarize it or, in other words, render play uncanny in the Freudian sense. The overall effect in *The Conjuring* is "making childish fun ironically synonymous with adult fear" (Lennard 2014, 131). Perhaps that is the strongest metaphor in the film – that the things we do and play in our youth is what haunts us in the future. Part of it also may tie into childhood sense of exclusion, competition, and even threats from play, which we do not necessarily outgrow as adults. Child's play is fun, but it is also serious business that can become terrifying, and in the universe of *The Conjuring*, often does.

WOMEN'S WORK

In such haunted house films as *The Haunting* (1963, Robert Wise) and *The Woman in Black* (2012, James Watkins), the nursery is connected to the house's traumatic history and becomes a locus of the haunting. Motherhood is often a vital aspect of haunted house films, and in particular wronged mothers or mothers who were deprived of their children (or conversely, children deprived of their mothers). *The Conjuring* is a film that, at heart, is centered on four mothers and their interactions with their children: Bathsheba Sherman, Mrs. Walker, Carolyn Perron and Lorraine Warren. Villain, victims and hero are all women and specifically all mothers. Motherhood in particular defines Carolyn Perron – she has five daughters and is a stay-at-home mom. This is in contrast to Roger Perron, whose work as a truck driver both sites him as the breadwinner of the family while also removing him from the house for long periods of time. Carolyn is thus responsible for the household while he is gone. Carolyn's life is rooted in domesticity and child-care, as opposed to Bathsheba Sherman and Mrs. Walker, mothers who killed their children.

Similarly, Lorraine Warren is a wife and mother, but the film distinguishes her from Carolyn. Lorraine has a daughter, but that daughter is often left in the care of a grandparent or family friend, meaning Lorraine is not a stay-at-home mom. Carolyn interacts constantly with her daughters and even seems to play regularly with April, the youngest child who is not yet in school. Lorraine and Ed are clearly presented as partners, the sign on the wall pronouncing "The Warrens: Consultants of Demonology, Witchcraft." Both husband and wife work together. Unlike Carolyn, Lorraine's sphere is not the domestic or child-care. Her relationship with Judy seems distant, almost strained. She loves her daughter but leaves childcare to the grandmother.

Women, particularly mothers, are also the characters most profoundly affected by the haunting. Carolyn becomes possessed, Lorraine has been damaged by the exorcism of Maurice, and it is the Perron girls who are the initial targets of the infestation. Judy is attacked by Annabelle and Bathsheba, who themselves are the cause of the haunting in the first place. Conversely, the men seem to get off easy.

Roger Perron is the one least affected by the house. His concerns are more mundane, more real, if one may use that term. Feeding five girls is expensive, he tells them. He is worried they cannot afford the mortgage on the house. If he does not get more routes he will lose first the insurance on his rig, then his rig. His fears are that of the *pater familias* – loss of the ability to care for, feed and shelter his family. He grows angry initially at the children and Carolyn's insistence that there is something wrong in the house. He seems to resent the Warren's intrusion. Not quite toxic masculinity, but rather a fear of loss of control and loss of his identity as the father. He is in a house with eight women – a wife, five daughters, the ghost of Bathsheba's first victim, and the demonic witch ghost out to destroy them all. Roger dismisses the assertions of supernatural causes of the weird things happening in part due to the youth of his children, but also, one might suspect, because they are girls. When Christine panics after seeing something behind the door in the dark, Roger asserts, "I'm pretty sure that it was just a bad dream."

One can read *The Conjuring* from a feminist perspective, in which case the film is rather conservative. Writing for *Salon*, Andrew O'Hehir objects to "the film's deeply reactionary cultural politics, and the profound misogyny that lurks just beneath its surface," arguing the film evokes the seventies not just in its setting but also in its politics (2013). This assertion is true, but the film is more nuanced than that. Women occupy the center of the film, and mothers are among the most important of the women. But each of the women in the film has a male figure to whom she is beholden and in some ways subservient. Although a partner to his wife, Roger is clearly the man of the house. Lorraine and Ed are partners, but as a male he's the one to carry out the exorcism, he is the one who takes the lead on the investigation. The irony is that Ed actually gets it wrong quite often. The exorcism fails and only Lorraine and Carolyn are able to exorcise Bathsheba. In the investigation it is Lorraine who figures out every aspect, from the presence of Bathsheba to the idea that she possesses the mother to kill the child. The men involved are neither as informed nor as useful as the women. Indeed, the clearest alpha male, Officer Brad, is also the figure of comic relief. He is clearly out of his element. Thus, I would argue the film might be reactionary, but has a much more complicated approach to gender than simple "misogyny."

On the one hand, resisting evil in the film becomes a matter of traditional values. The film values the Warrens' traditional Catholicism, focusing on the power of Latin prayers, priestly blessings and the rituals of faith. Ed tells Roger to "get your children baptized," and holds up his own faith as a model both in public (at lectures) and in private (to Roger). The emphasis on marriage and the gendered roles within marriage in the film is obvious. Yet it is the women who drive the film. Indeed, there is a tension in the feminine in the film, between empowering women while simultaneously ensuring that power is limited, so the patriarchal, heteronormative family is preserved and protected.

Bathsheba represents a subversive element in all this, because she is a mother who rejects motherhood and pushes other women to do the same – a woman who is a threat to male dominance, not easily beaten by men. She is a threat to the patriarchy, although one might also note that she is still in the service of Satan, so even the powerful witch is subservient to a figure traditionally coded as male. In the end, however, she is defeated by Lorraine – a mother and wife who subscribes to and supports the patriarchy and often defers to her husband and the Catholic Church. Thus, it is the ghosts and demons in the film that become the voice of feminism, which is not necessarily misogynistic either.

Robin Roberts reminds us that female ghosts "expose the ways that the feminine is silenced and constrained" (2018, 6). Supernatural powers allow the ghost to overcome obstacles not possible to overcome while alive. The Bathsheba of the film rejected motherhood and marriage. She became more powerful in death than she was in life. Similarly, Mrs. Walker was easily duped into killing her own child by Bathsheba, but we know nothing of Mr. Walker. The woman is the victim or the monster, but in being either she exposes the hypocrisy beneath the patriarchy. In the end, though, Bathsheba remains a monster who must be stopped.

Roberts further observes that the job of the maternal ghost is to "terrify other parents and kill children," which ties Bathsheba to other such ghost monster mothers, such as the ones in *The Woman in Black* and *Mama* (2018, 13). Denied a satisfactory life, oppressed by men, the maternal ghost is a revolutionary against traditional gender roles, seeking to fight against the very social structures that oppressed her. Bathsheba attempts a kind of feminine solidarity – she is able to convince Mrs. Walker to kill Rory, and then herself, just as Bathsheba did, and she wants Carolyn Perron to kill her daughters, and then, presumably, herself. Bathsheba disrupts the family unit and ends the father-dominated nuclear family model.

Julia Kristeva's *Powers of Horror: An Essay on Abjection* theorizes the state of the abject, that which exists on the boundary between categories. She argues that women, in particular, exist in a state of abjection, and that it is the maternal body that manifests the abject in its purest form. It is "desirable and terrifying, nourishing and murderous, fascinating and abject" (1982, 54). In the womb the child is a part of the mother; outside the womb it is a separate being. The film focuses on the damage being done to Carolyn Perron's body by the slow possession, beginning with a bruise she mistakenly believes she received during lovemaking with Roger on the first night of the house and ending with her face utterly transformed into Bathsheba's during the exorcism. Her body as a mother is abject, is the locus of desire and yet is also the murderous instrument which might end April and Christine if given the chance. It is not Carolyn doing this; it is Bathsheba in Carolyn's body.

After killing her child, Bathsheba hanged herself, which absolves society of the guilt that would have resulted from her wrongful death. Many of the accounts of Salem focus on the injustice of the execution of innocent women at the hands of a male-controlled judicial system. Bathsheba was not hanged by men; she was killed by a woman, by herself. The film indicates that she was not punished unjustly, as the Salem witches were. She was not a victim of the patriarchy or a patriarchal culture. She is rather a malevolent woman who seeks to destroy other families. This is in contrast to the Warrens, who repeatedly assert they were "brought together by God." Bathsheba, the godless, empowered, childless mother is defeated by the heteronormative, faith-having, traditional married couple.

In short, *The Conjuring* is female-centric; it is not, however, particularly feminist.

Chapter Four: "Everything You See in Here is Either Haunted, Cursed, or Has Been Used in Some Kind of Ritualistic Practice." Or, The Endless *Conjuring* Universe

THE *CONJURING* UNIVERSE

The Conjuring does not have sequels. It has a "universe."[2] Not unlike the superhero films of Marvel or DC, *The Conjuring* has sparked an entire group of loosely linked films that are now considered to be taking place within the same shared universe. They are loosely linked by the narratives of the Warrens, the doll Annabelle, and the demon Valak (whose preferred form seems to be a spooky nun). Even *The Curse of La Llorona*, which is seemingly only tangentially linked to the series through Father Perez, who appeared in *Annabelle* and who mentions the Warrens in passing to Anna, telling her he knows of a couple on the East coast who deal with situations like hers, is actually linked to the other films in the series not only narratively, but through a shared aesthetic – muted colors, long tracking shots, use of darkness and light to create tension, etc. – shared culture, and common tropes. This chapter will consider the parents and children of *The Conjuring* and the different elements that unite the series.

All of the films in the *Conjuring* Universe have a shared culture. They are rooted in the 1970s, with flashbacks to the fifties and sixties: times of radical transition within the United States and within the Catholic Church. As noted in chapter two, Vatican II radically changed Catholicism, both in terms of its approach to the world as well as its everyday practice. Mass was no longer said in Latin but in the vernacular. The priest faced the congregation rather than the altar. Included in this transformation were sweeping aesthetic changes. Nuns were no longer required to wear habits (echoed in the tension of Sister Irene not wearing her formal habit in *The Nun*) and ornate clerical regalia was discouraged. Music, art and architecture were transformed in the wake of the council, further reflected in the material culture of Catholicism. Prayers, the calendar and the structure of mass were changed. Greater roles for the laity were allowed, most strongly evinced in the films by Ed and Lorraine Warren serving as the voice of the Church in *The Conjuring* and *The Conjuring 2*. All of these changes can see seen reflected in *The Conjuring* Universe.

The changes were not merely in the Church. The social fabric shifted during this period: changes in divorce laws made it easier for marriages to end and divorce rates rose (single mothers appear in *The Conjuring 2* and *The Curse of La Llorona*; although in the case of the latter Anna is a widow, still the single-parent household became more of a reality in the seventies), abortion became legal in the United States after the Supreme Court decided Roe v. Wade in 1973. The late sixties and early seventies saw disillusionment grow amongst the American public for major institutions, particularly after the escalation of the conflict in Vietnam and the resistance to both the war and the draft at home, the Civil Rights movement, the backlash against it and the assassinations of John F. Kennedy, Dr. Martin Luther King Jr., and Robert Kennedy, as well as the sexual revolution and the Women's Rights Movement. The massacre at Kent State, the riots in Watts in 1965 and at the 1968 Democratic National Convention, and the Tate-LaBianca murders by the Manson cult in 1969 are all signifiers, among many, of the social and cultural turbulence which marked the period. The original *Conjuring* captures a traditional family living on the outskirts of all these social changes. *The Conjuring* Universe echoes that turbulence indirectly. Let us consider what elements are shared by the films in *The Conjuring* Universe.

THE CONJURING UNIVERSE IS A SUPERNATURAL UNIVERSE

In addition to the supernatural reality espoused in the original film's Catholicism, all films in the *Conjuring* Universe feature ghosts and demons that are demonstrably real and have efficacy in the real world. They can hurt, they can destroy, and they can kill. They are both visible and invisible and almost universally what they seek is first to terrify and then to possess or destroy. These entities are genuinely evil. They are not misunderstood, they are not the embodiment of cultural difference, they are not mistaken. They are evil and seek to do evil in the world. The same entities recur throughout the series. The doll Annabelle and the entity that uses it as a conduit is present in five of the seven films to date (*The Conjuring, Annabelle, Annabelle: Creation, The Curse Of La Llorona*, and *Annabelle Comes Home*), the demon Valak, who appears blasphemously as a nun, is present in three (*The Conjuring 2, Annabelle: Creation* and *The Nun*). Historically, Valak is a demon described in the goetic grimoire *The Lesser Key of Solomon*, a mid-seventeenth century anonymous book on demonology, and other, similar texts, as a winged, angelic-looking boy riding a two-headed dragon (Peterson 2001, 35; 248). He can tell where treasure is hidden and where serpents are, and commands thirty legions of demons. The entity in *The Conjuring* universe bears no relationship to this actual demon.

We might note, Protestant theology does not typically allow for ghosts or the spirits of the dead. Of the 108 times the word "ghost" is used in the King James Bible, it always refers to either the Holy Ghost or to someone "giving up the ghost," not once to a disembodied spirit remaining on earth after death. Multiple scriptures note that ghosts are not possible: "As the cloud disappears and vanishes away, so he who goes down to the grave does not come up. He shall never return to his house, nor shall his place know him anymore" (Job 7:9-10). Or, "For the living know that they will die; But the dead know nothing, and they have no more reward, For the memory of them is forgotten. Also, their love, their hatred, and their envy have now perished; nevermore will they have a share in anything done under the sun" (Ecclesiastes 9:5-6). Hebrews 9:27 suggests after death, the soul is sent immediately to heaven or hell, leaving no room for the possibility of disembodied spirits roaming the earth. All of these contribute to the Protestant belief that ghosts are not theologically possible.

However, scripture is also ambiguous on the ability to communicate with the dead: "And when they say to you, 'Consult the mediums and the spiritists who whisper and mutter.' Should not a people consult their God? Should they consult the dead on behalf of the living?" (Isaiah 8:19). Leviticus 19:31 states, "Give no regard to mediums and familiar spirits; do not seek after them, to be defiled by them: I am the LORD your God." One can only be defiled by something that actually is. 1 John 4:1,4 seems to warn of wicked spirits: "Beloved, do not believe every spirit, but test the spirits, whether they are of God... You are of God, little children, and have overcome them, because He who is in you is greater than he who is in the world." Likewise, in the Hebrew Bible, King Saul uses a medium (referred to as the Witch of Endor) to communicate with the dead spirit of God's prophet Samuel (1 Samuel 28:7-20). Deuteronomy 18:11 forbids "consulting with familiar spirits." In other words, the Bible is self-contradictory about whether or not ghosts are possible.

Catholicism allows for the possibility of communication with the dead through the Communion of Saints. According to the *Catechism of the Catholic Church*, "Our prayers for [the dead] are capable not only of helping them, but also of making their intercession for us effective" (1994, 958). In other words, in Catholicism, there can be interaction between the living and the souls of the dead, as well as with demonic entities. Catholicism also allows for the possibility of exorcism as outlined in the Roman Ritual and familiar to many from horror movies.

Linked to its Catholicism, therefore, the *Conjuring* Universe recognizes the reality of spiritual evil and the many forms it takes. One need not be Catholic or a believer in the supernatural in order to find these films frightening. But the films are linked by their assertion of the reality of demons, ghosts and other supernatural entities, almost all of which are evil in nature and must be combated by forces of good, such as the Warrens, Rafael, Father Perez, and Sister Irene. In the absence of such figures, evil wins, as we see happen in *Annabelle: Creation*, in which Janice is possessed, vanishes and re-emerges as "Annabelle," who is adopted and grows up to kill her parents, or in *The Conjuring 2*, which opens with Ronnie DeFeo killing his family as witnessed by Lorraine.

THE CONJURING UNIVERSE IS A ROMAN CATHOLIC UNIVERSE

Even when it gets Catholicism demonstrably wrong (such as in *Annabelle: Creation* when Janice gives her confession to Sister Charlotte – nuns are not allowed to receive confession or grant absolution for sins, something that would have been known by both characters in the period), the world of *The Conjuring* is a demonstrably Catholic one. Yet, as the error above shows, the Catholicism of *The Conjuring* Universe is a cultural and material one far more than a theological one. It is a universe filled with old abbeys and convents, church buildings, priests and nuns, crucifixes and prayers in Latin. Missing from this universe is any theology other than demonology. Father Perez, witnessing a smudging, says to Anna when she asks if he believes in its efficacy: "What I believe doesn't matter; it's what they believe. And if they believe in that, they surely believe in this [indicates the Catholic Church building]." This attitude is both an echo of the ecumenicism found in Catholicism after the Second Vatican Council and also of the *ad hoc* Catholicism of the films. Lorraine's clairvoyance, Father Perez's respect for and

Rafael's use of traditional rituals, and the various items in the Warren's occult museum indicate a belief in preternatural and supernatural entities, events, and powers that lie outside traditional Catholicism.

The people of the *Conjuring* universe are Catholic, and they affiliate strongly with clergy. Father Gordon (and Father Perez of the *Annabelle* films) serves as a conduit to the official Church. Ed and Lorraine Warren, however, are also presented as the embodiment of a living Catholic faith, using relics, icons and crucifixes to combat the supernatural, reciting prayers from the *Rituale Romanum*, and advocating strongly for baptism and the sacraments, as well as the importance of faith itself. Even Rafael Olvera, the traditional healer in *The Curse of La Llorona*, is a former Catholic priest. *The Nun* is anchored by Father Burke and Sister Irene, as well as numerous other nuns, living and dead. The people, beliefs and material culture of *The Conjuring* films are Roman Catholic in nature, if not directly, as is its theology.

THE CONJURING UNIVERSE IS A FEMALE-CENTRIC UNIVERSE

As noted in the previous chapter, *The Conjuring* films feature women as the heroes, victims and monsters. While a feminist critique of the film suggests that it is female-centric but not feminist, the films all center around women. Mothers are especially central to the *Conjuring* Universe in all three roles. *The Conjuring* features four mothers, Carolyn, Lorraine, Mrs. Walker, and Bathsheba. All four women have children. Bathsheba and Walker have killed theirs; Lorraine places hers in danger, and Carolyn, possessed by Bathsheba, attempts to kill two of her children. The Warrens have a daughter, Judy, and five women make up the Perron children. We might also note that Lorraine is the one with actual powers, and the one who eventually helps Carolyn drive Bathsheba out. Ed might be a demonologist, but it is Lorraine who has the abilities and who has the greatest impact on the Perron family. It is worth noting that Ed's exorcism fails, but Lorraine is able to talk to Carolyn and then Carolyn herself fights against and expels Bathsheba. Unlike in all previous exorcism films, *The Conjuring* shows that women, not men, have the power to drive out possessing forces.

The first film is remarkably filled with a variety of strong female characters, and so are all the subsequent entries in this universe. *Annabelle* centers on Mia as a mother, Leah, her newborn daughter, the daughter of the next-door neighbors who kills her parents and attempts to kill Mia and, of course, Annabelle herself. *The Conjuring 2* is again dominated by its female characters, from the antagonistic nun (Valak in female form) who controls Bill, the ghost in the house, the spiritually afflicted Janet and Peggy Hodgson, and, of course, Lorraine, who saves her husband Ed and Janet from Valek. In *Annabelle: Creation* we again see women dominate the story: Bee, whose death results in the creation of (and naming of) Annabelle, the tormented Esther, orphaned sisters Linda and Janice, as well as the other four girls in the Mullins House (Carol, Nancy, Kate and Tierney), and Sister Charlotte, their protector and spiritual advisor. The men in this film are ineffective and clueless – Father Massey is unaware of the danger of Annabelle, offering the doll to the girls at the end of the film. Samuel Mullins brings the orphans into his house to atone for what has happened, but he actually is leading lambs to the slaughter as he knows there is an evil presence in the house. He himself is killed by Annabelle.

Women are at the center of *The Nun*, from the eponymous entity to Sister Irene, who defeats Valak when the men fail. There are a number of other nuns who fight the evil in the Abbey of St. Carta, most notably Sister Victoria, who sacrifices herself rather than let Valak take her soul and thereby enter the world. Father Burke and Frenchie, the two male characters, are defeated by Valak, and Frenchie becomes the means by which Valak finally is able to enter the world. In *The Nun*, women fight and defeat evil, men are at best ineffective against it and at worst act as the conduit through which it can manifest. Similarly, in *The Curse of La Llorona*, Anna, the protagonist, is a single mother who must fight against a demonic mother, La Llorona herself. Along the way she inadvertently allows the sons of Patricia to be killed by La Llorona, resulting in Patricia attempting to help La Llorona take Anna's children in hopes of having her own returned. In this film three mothers fight to either hurt or help children, while men attempt to help, but again prove only slightly effective. Rafael helps Anna and her family, but Anna is the one who defeats the entity. Lastly, *Annabelle Comes Home*, like *Annabelle: Creation*, revolves primarily around a group of young women encountering the supernatural. Although the Warrens are present at the beginning and end of the film, their presence bookends the heart of it: Judy Warren, Mary Ellen, and Daniela fight the spirits that Daniela inadvertently releases when she enters the occult museum. Annabelle herself, a "beacon for other spirits" is oddly also a strong female presence in the film, helping to animate haunted armor, a haunted television set, and summon a ghost werewolf. In short, women dominate *The Conjuring* Universe as protagonists, antagonists and the primary movers of the story. Mothers in particular are at the center of the universe, but young women and even girls are also given a place of prominence.

The monstrous women of *The Conjuring* Universe are part of a larger trend of predatory female monsters in the twenty-first century, most notable from American adaptations of J-horror in such films as *The Ring* (2002, Gore Verbinski), *The Grudge* (2004, Shimizu Takashi), *One Missed Call* (2008, Eric Valette), and *Shutter* (2008, Masayuki Ochiai), and in later American supernatural horror films such as Mrs. Ganush in *Drag Me to Hell* (2009, Sam Raimi), Mama in *Mama*, Diana in *Lights Out*, and Sue Ann AKA "Ma" in *Ma* (2019, Tate Taylor). Such "monsters" can be perceived as feminist figures, threats to male authority and power; countered only by equally strong female heroes. *The Conjuring* Universe connects strongly to this trend, and in doing so is thus profoundly female-centric, both for its "good guys" and "bad guys," most of whom are not actually guys at all. The tension of these films is that they put women in the center, even though they still deliver a conservative narrative that reinforces many ideas of the patriarchy.

THE PARENTS AND CHILDREN OF *THE CONJURING*

INSIDIOUS (2010)

In some ways, *Insidious* is a forerunner of *The Conjuring*, engaging some of the same themes and sharing a sensibility when it comes to horror and the depiction of the supernatural. Not only do both films share the presence of Patrick Wilson as performer and James Wan as director, they also share a house with a supernatural presence that masks a more challenging entity. Written by longtime Wan associate Leigh Whannell, who also scripted *Saw* and *Dead Silence* (another film that presages *The Conjuring*), *Insidious*, like *The Conjuring*, features a family, the Lamberts, who come under the sway of the supernatural, resulting in the need to ask experts in the paranormal to help end the horror; in this case, psychic Elise Rainier (Lin Shaye) and her assistants, Specs and Tucker.

Insidious sets the mode for Wan's style of ghost story, especially since this ghost story is not a traditional ghost story at all, although it begins with all the hallmarks of one. The film reveals that it is not the house that's haunted, it is the family. The entity that is most dangerous in *Insidious* is not the demon that kidnaps the soul of young Dalton as he astral projects; it is the old woman who stalked Josh as a child and has now come for his son. Indeed, at the end of the film, it is Josh that is possessed and Dalton who is freed. Linking this film with its descendent is this notion that the family is haunted and thus it is impossible to leave (see Murphy 2015). Part of the horror of *Insidious* is that the family cannot escape it. Elise tells the family if they move (again) the spirits will just continue to follow them. "It's not the house that's haunted," she earnestly intones, "it's you." The warning is repeated by the Warrens to the Perrons in *The Conjuring*. If the Perrons leave the farmhouse, Bathsheba will only follow them. This idea will continue through *The Conjuring* Universe – Valak is both in the Warren house and in the Hodgson Enfield flat, as well as the Abbey of St. Carta. The Amityville house allegedly told the priest to "get out" (tangentially inspiring the Jordan Peele film of that name), and all one had to do was leave the house and the horror stopped. The monsters of *Insidious* and *The Conjuring*, however, follow you. Similarly, both families, the Lamberts and the Perrons, are unable to move again because of economic issues. They simply cannot afford to move to a house that is not haunted; they remained trapped in the house. (See also Murphy 2015 for more thinking in this vein.)

What separates *Insidious* from *The Conjuring* is The Further, the astral realm in which the former's spirits and demons dwell. The horror of *Insidious* is the idea of being trapped in The Further while someone or something else occupies your body. The representation of The Further, however, is echoed in the various dark spaces of *The Conjuring* universe: in the cellar of the Perron farmhouse, in the barn in *Annabelle: Creation*, and in the Warren home in *Annabelle Comes Home*. In all three films, light cast goes no further than the person holding the light source.

Lastly, *Insidious* also shares the success of *The Conjuring*. Budgeted at approximately $1.5 million, *Insidious* earned global box-office receipts of $97 upon its initial release and inspired a series of sequels creating its own universe centered around "The Further": *Insidious, Chapter 2* (2013), *Insidious, Chapter 3* (2015) – a prequel that, like *Annabelle*, gives the backstory for the first film, in this case the history of Elise Rainier – and *Insidious: The Last Key* (2018), a sequel to the prequel that gives more of Rainier's history.

ANNABELLE (2014)

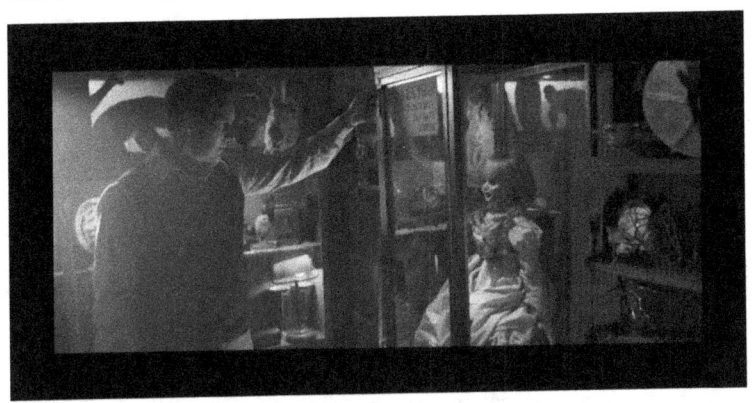

The breakout star of The Conjuring *was Annabelle – featured in three films of her own.*

Although the doll was tangential to the action in *The Conjuring*, "Annabelle" served as an early and eerie scare for the audience and ended up being popular enough that a film about her appeared before *The Conjuring 2*. According to producer Peter Safran, the question the filmmakers wanted to ask was, "How does something so charming, so sweet, become a conduit for pure evil and destruction?" (Campus Circle 2014, 14). Although it should be noted that the doll in the film seems anything but charming and sweet, even before it became the conduit for pure evil and destruction. The porcelain doll is creepy from the very beginning.

Set in 1967, the film tells the origin for the doll, which was originally a gift for expectant mother Mia Form from her husband John. They name it Annabelle. One night, the neighbor's house is invaded by their estranged daughter, now a member of a satanic cult, and her boyfriend. The parents are killed and the couple goes next door to kill John and Mia. The daughter dies holding the doll in her lap. After this, strange things begin happening in the Form household – the sewing machine runs on its own, the television continually loses reception, and Annabelle's rocking chair moves on its own.

John throws Annabelle away at Mia's request, but the doll returns. Mia gives birth to a daughter named Leah, and the doll menaces both mother and newborn. At one point Annabelle appears to be levitating, but Mia sees the actual entity behind it, holding it in the air (in a scene reminiscent of *Insidious*). Eventually, Father Perez, their parish priest, becomes involved and eventually takes Annabelle from them. "At the very least," he tells them, "I've heard of a married couple that the Church has worked with in the past that deals with this type of thing. They're back east, but a call can always be placed," a clear reference to the Warrens, although they would not become involved in Annabelle's story until the doll ended up with the nurses in *The Conjuring*. The question must then be asked, how did Annabelle end up in a thrift store if Father Perez took the doll and planned on calling the Warrens? The other implication, however, is that the Warrens were destined to cross paths with the possessed doll at some point.

Sadly, however, as one might infer from the plot summary above, the film has little actually happen in it, certainly compared to *The Conjuring*, and lacks tension. Slow and devoid of dread, this film is disconnected from much of *The Conjuring* Universe narrative.

The Conjuring 2 (2016)

"After everything we've seen, there isn't much that rattles either of us anymore. But this one… this one still haunts me," Lorraine's voiceover informs the audience, promising an even more terrifying recounting than the events in Rhode Island.

Just as *The Conjuring* began with an unrelated case, *Conjuring 2* begins with a séance in Amityville before proceeding to the actual narrative: the Enfield poltergeist case. This film is even less accurate than the first in terms of the history of the case. The definitive book on the Enfield poltergeist, *This House Is Haunted*, by Guy Lyon Playfair who, with Maurice Grosse was one of two lead investigators at Enfield for the Society for Psychical Research, does not even mention the Warrens (Playfair 1980).[3] By all accounts, the Warrens were present for only a day or two (although Ed claims they stayed for a week [Brittle 1980, 223]). The Warrens shared their version of the Enfield poltergeist in Gerald Brittle's *The Demonologist*, the title of which refers to Ed Warren. In chapter fourteen, "The Enfield Voices," there is a transcript of a conversation with "Fred", the spirit that conducts much of the conversation between Janet as possessed by Bill and Ed as seen in the film, although the Warrens claim the conversation was not with a possessed girl but with voices that spoke in the room. Regardless of how much the

Warrens were actually involved in the Enfield poltergeist case, Ed claimed, "The Enfield case makes Amityville look like a playhouse," a point the film repeats several times (Brittle 1980, 222). The film also continually draws links between Enfield and Amityville, from the opening séance to the talk show to the several references to it.

In some ways, *The Conjuring 2* is not just a sequel title but a description of the film itself, which echoes many elements of the first. As noted above, the film begins with an unrelated case that will end up impacting the main narrative. Both films employ on-screen text to assert the truth of the events depicted, and give Ed and Lorraine the opportunity to demonstrate they are honest about what is a haunting and what is not. They depict an economically disenfranchised but not truly poor family under siege from supernatural forces (the Perrons and the Hodgsons), providing the impetus for the Warrens to come and fight a demonic evil. And in both films one of the Warrens is afraid for the well-being of the other and does not want them involved in the case. The supernatural elements and the family's response to it in the first film are also echoed in the second, from bed linens being pulled off and the appearance of apparitions to the family all sleeping together in the same room for safety.

The opening in Amityville visually echoes Wan's work in *Insidious*, in which Lorraine's spirit leaves her body and looks back and sees herself, just as Patrick Wilson's character did in *Insidious*. Lorraine is able to witness Ronnie DeFeo murder his family in their sleep, allegedly the inciting incident for the Amityville haunting, later considered to be a hoax by many. Lorraine is also shown a vision of Ed being killed, driving her to echo Ed in the first film, wanting him not to participate in fear he will be killed somehow by a supernatural entity.

A crawl follows, text on the screen linking Amityville to Enfield, and once again asserting, "This is a True Story." The action moves to the United Kingdom where a working-class family living in a terrace house begins to experience the supernatural. In this film as well we see Wan's moving camera active from the beginning. In a single tracking shot, the street is shown. A car drives by the camera, which moves with the car as it then enters the yard of the house to the right of the street before rising up to a window, travelling through the glass and into the boys' room, continuing down the hall to where a mother and child stand by a child's fort at the end of the hall. With a single tracking shot, Wan has brought the audience into the heart of the house, implying both a voyeuristic impulse on the part of the viewer and that the entity is free to move about the home.

Ed and Lorraine appear on a talk show to discuss Amityville in which a fellow guest, a skeptic relying upon condescension and baseless accusations instead of evidence, claims that Amityville was a hoax and Ed and Lorraine are charlatans. Ed defends their work and the film clearly supports Ed's interpretation of events and belief in the supernatural. Just as in the original film, in which Ed and Lorraine tell a suburban couple their home is not haunted and that there are very few real hauntings, this film presents a bit of a straw man counter to the Warrens so that they can demonstrate that they are rational and sincere, so that when they say a haunting is real we can believe them, because, the films seem to say, they would tell us if they were not.

In this film, the Hodgsons, a single-parent, four-child family in Enfield, is ostensibly haunted by "Bill," a former resident of the home. Janet Hodgson, one of the daughters, becomes possessed by Bill. Across the Atlantic, Ed paints a terrifying nun (a callback to his own early career as an amateur painter) which Lorraine begins seeing in dreams and visions.[1] As the Warrens investigate, they realize that just as Rory and Mrs. Walker in the first film were merely spirits under threat from the more demonic Bathsheba, Bill is a mere puppet of Valak, a demon that uses the Hodgsons to attack the Warrens.

The music box of the first film is replaced by the "Crooked Man" toy, which also plays a song and serves as a conduit for a spirit – in this case "the Crooked Man" himself, a manifestation of evil as a sort of cartoon monstrous man. Bathsheba is here replaced by the demonic nun. A fight between the Warrens and the demonic entity at the climax of the film sees the Warren's faith helping them to defeat the demon and free the family from the supernatural threat with no permanent damage to Ed and Lorraine either. As in the first film, the end credits juxtapose images of the actual people involved with the names of the actors playing them, accompanied by the actual recording of Ed interviewing a possessed Janet. This buttresses the assertion that the film depicts real events.

Wan and the Hayes brothers wrote the screenplay and Wan directed the sequel, and thus the film feels like a replication of the first. The word most often used to describe it in reviews was "bloated," and it was not as well received. Tomris Laffly observes the film feels "curiously emotionally vacant" unlike the first, stating, "if *The Conjuring* was a flawlessly executed, hearty dish that followed a timeless, classic recipe, this feels like an attempt to deconstruct and fancy it up, to prove something that no one necessarily asked for" (2016). This observation rings true – if the first film is, as I have argued here, a well-constructed magic trick, then seeing the trick repeated does not add to it.

Tangentially, the year before *The Conjuring 2* was released, British Sky Broadcasting produced and released a three-episode miniseries also based on the Enfield poltergeist case. Guy Lyon Playfair consulted for the series, which was based upon his book, Timothy Spall played Maurice Grosse (played by Simon McBurney in *The Conjuring 2*), and the story is radically different. Neither the Warrens nor Valak were present in the BSkyB series (perhaps a result of an ongoing legal dispute).

ANNABELLE: CREATION (2017)

The problem with *Annabelle: Creation* is that Annabelle has already had two creation stories – one in *The Conjuring* and one in *Annabelle*. This third one does not mesh with the others. In *The Conjuring* two student nurses have a doll that was a gift to one of them from her mother. Debbie, the doll's recipient, tells Ed and Lorraine, "Camilla got in touch with a medium. We learned from her that a 7-year-old-girl named Annabelle Higgins had died in this apartment. She was lonely and took a liking to my doll. All she wanted was to be friends." The nurses thus "gave her permission to move into the doll." Camilla, the other nurse, tells Ed and Lorraine, "She wanted to live with us by inhabiting the doll." Ed and Lorraine then explain there is no Annabelle; some demonic entity was lying to gain access to their souls – the doll is a mere conduit. Before her death, the doll was just a creepy doll, nothing more. *Annabelle* offers another creation story – the doll is invested with the spirit of a young cult member who killed her parents and is then killed holding the doll when she invades the house next door. *Annabelle: Creation*, however, posits a variant on the first story and adds to the second. Samuel and Esther Mullins, after losing their daughter in an accident, invited what they thought was her spirit into a doll that Samuel had made. It is implied that an intervention followed to save Mrs. Mullins, in much the same manner as with Carolyn in *The Conjuring*, and the entity remained attached to the doll ever since.

The question then is: did the entity attach itself to the doll when the Mullins invited it in, when the cultist died holding the doll in the Form house, or when the nurses invited it into the doll? These three stories are not mutually exclusive but do indicate a complicated existence for the doll. If all three are true, what drove the spirit out of the doll each time requiring it to manipulate its way back into the doll?

What is interesting about *Annabelle: Creation* is that it is a prequel to a prequel, with scenes that take place in 1943, 1952, 1955, and 1967, meaning it takes place before and after *The Nun* and its closing scene connects it to *Annabelle*. A stronger and better-made film than either its predecessor or successor (indeed, in ranking the films of *The Conjuring* Universe, critic William Bibbiani ranks *Annabelle: Creation* second only to the original *Conjuring*, and finds it a "rollercoaster of a horror film…that finally does the creepy doll proud" [2018]). Director David S. Sandberg creates tension and suspense in much the same manner as Wan did while still offering a new narrative with its own sources of anxiety and dread. It is arguably the best-reviewed *Conjuring* universe film since the original.

The film opens with a montage of Annabelle being assembled by the Biblically-named toymaker Samuel Mullins. He brands the interior of the doll – this is a limited edition and he has just made the first of one hundred. He and his also Biblically-named wife Esther lose their daughter Annabelle, called "Bee" for short, in an accident after attending church (she is struck by a car when her father stops by the side of the road to repair a flat tire). Years later, they open their Southern California desert home to six orphan girls, including sisters Janice, who was stricken with polio and has a leg brace and a wheelchair, and Linda, and Sister Charlotte, their guardian, a Catholic nun who is from the same order as the sisters at the Abbey of St. Carta in *The Nun*. (Tangentially, Sister Charlotte has a black and white photo of herself with three of the other nuns from the abbey, and visible in the photo, at the side behind them is Valak in nun form, setting up both the forthcoming *The Nun* and the link to *The Conjuring 2*, firmly cementing all of these films together as being in the same universe.) Abandoned by Linda, who plays with the other girls, running around the property, Janice plays in Bee's old bedroom where she finds Annabelle, locked in a closet covered in pages from the Bible, among other remarkable toys created by Samuel. Bee's bedroom is off-limits, a shrine to her memory, but Janice finds in it a world in which she can play freely, an activity much more challenging when she is with her able-bodied friends.

From Annabelle's first discovery by Janice, her presence is a spooky one. Janice throws a blanket over Annabelle and the covered figure stands up and begins following her. When the blanket finally falls off, nothing is there (echoing the theme found in *The Conjuring* of the scariest things being those you cannot see). The girls explore the property, discovering a sinister scarecrow in the barn that will threaten them later. Linda discovers Annabelle in a crawlspace below the stairs. What makes the moment genuinely terrifying is that for the first time we see the entity that actually is manipulating the doll. In the dark, Linda (and the audience) can make out a malevolent face with glowing eyes holding the doll, and then whisking it out of sight. The entity, or parts of it, will be seen a few more times in the film – the only time the thing that has "never walked the earth in human form" is visible, rather than just Annabelle the doll. More and more mysterious events begin to frighten all six girls. Nancy and Carol sit under a sheet with a flashlight making up stories about Mrs. Mullins, making fun of her. Mrs. Mullin's bell then rings and the flashlight goes out. Something is in the room with them, attacking them beneath the sheet. Janice and Linda play in Bee's room when the ghost of Bee appears, before turning into a demon and then black mist.

Eventually, Janice is possessed by the demon that uses Annabelle as a conduit, which then murders Mr. Mullins. The film's point of view then shifts to Linda who is the only one who realizes there is something wrong with Janet. Linda throws Annabelle down the well on the property, but something in the well grabs her, and only the arrival of Sister Charlotte prevents her from being taken. Esther then tells Sister Charlotte how Annabelle came to be, which is virtually the same story told by the nurses in *The Conjuring*. Bee's ghost appeared to her parents and asked if she could move into the doll and still be with them. It was too late when they realized it was not their daughter, but rather something pretending to be her. "It was a demonic presence, and it was using our Annabelle to manipulate us into giving it a soul it could inhabit. It tried to take mine but Samuel reached out to the Church. They saved my soul, but the evil was still attached to that doll." As with previous films, it is the Church, the fathers and the men that must step in and save the women from themselves and the demonic. And, as with previous films, in the end the men who step in are ultimately proven ineffectual at actually stopping the evil: spoiler alert! Annabelle will escape and Father Massey is presented as clueless as to the actual nature of the doll.

The demon attached to the doll finally launches an all-out assault on the household, trapping Carol in the barn with the scary scarecrow, crucifying Mrs. Mullins' torso on the wall and chasing Linda throughout the house, with Linda hiding from Janice in the one place she cannot look – the Scripture-covered room in which Annabelle was first found. Sister Charlotte attempts to use the tools of faith to fight the entity, placing a rosary over Janice's head and putting both Annabelle and Janet into the scripture-covered closet. When the door is opened, Annabelle and the rosary are there and Janet has vanished. Father Massey, the priest who supports the orphan community pronounces that while the doll was a conduit for evil, now "the doll is just a doll."

In the final scene, Janet, now calling herself Annabelle, is adopted from a different orphanage by the Higgins family, who are the neighbors to the Forms in *Annabelle*. They give her a big Raggedy Ann doll, a reference to the actual, historic Annabelle doll. Twelve years later, Janet (or now Annabelle) is the Higgins daughter who joined the satanic cult and returns with her boyfriend to kill her parents and then attempt to kill the Forms. Instead, she dies with the Annabelle doll in her lap and once again the evil is attached to the doll. After the credits there is a stinger set at the Abbey of St. Carta in Romania, 1953, in which a door opens and a faceless nun glides forward extinguishing candles: a clear advertisement for *The Nun*.

While second only to *The Conjuring* in this series, there is a missed opportunity in this film to explore the dynamics of being an orphan, and the relationship between families and the spaces they occupy, as well as to explore the anxieties of female adolescence. In terms of theme and character, a stronger and more interesting film lurks inside this one. Having said that, the film is beautifully shot and the predominantly young cast generates both empathy (and therefore tension when they are in danger) and terror (possessed Janice is rather frightening, perhaps even more so than possessed Carolyn Perron).

THE NUN (2018)

The problem of *The Nun* is that ultimately the activities of the titular character are purposeless, other than to frighten the audience. We learn in the opening sequence that Valak the Defiler, the Profane, the Marquis of Snakes, needs a vessel to escape his prison in the bowels of the Abbey of St. Carta. That is why Sister Victoria hangs herself – so that her body would not become possessed and allow Valak to leave the convent. The abbey was built by the Duke of St. Carta in the Dark Ages. Sister Oana tells Sister Irene: "He wrote countless texts on witchcraft and rituals, in which to call upon the forces of hell. Hell used him to open a gateway so that an unspeakable evil would walk amongst us." The church took over the building and had the nuns pray perpetually to keep the portal sealed. The bombs of the Second World War re-opened the portal and Valak stalks the halls in the form of a nun, seeking to corrupt. One must then ask – why all the illusions? Why the burial of Father Burke? Why stalk the halls at night, when no one is there? None of the nun's activities advance Valak's agenda. The point of *The Nun* seems to be twofold. The first is that it is simply a gothic adventure – a good-old fashioned jump scare movie set in *The Conjuring* Universe. When examined closely it is neither logical nor particularly dread-inducing in the way other films in the series are. The second is that it provides the backstory for the key evil in *The Conjuring 2*. In other words, like many horror series, later installments entirely rewrite the story so that there is new information about why the monster does what it does (see, for example, the *Halloween* and *Nightmare on Elm Street* series, in which Michael and Freddy, respectively, are given increasingly complicated and nonsensical backstories in order to expand the story). *The Nun* reinforces the Warrens-versus-demons through line of the series, both generally and specifically.

We learn that comic guide Frenchy's real name is Maurice Theriault. He is actually mentioned in *The Conjuring* when Ed and Lorraine deliver a lecture at Massachusetts Western University and show footage of his exorcism years after the events of *The Nun*. On the one hand, this connects *The Nun* more firmly to the first film, showing how Frenchie's experiences in Romania opened him to supernatural influence that would eventually bring him into contact with the Warrens. This perhaps seems a bit forced but if we take it at surface value, the implication is both that *The Conjuring* Universe is a small one and once one comes into contact with the demonic, it continues to impact and influence one's entire life. The larger implication is that in the same year the Warrens founded the New England Society for Psychic Research (1952), Valak was already working to enter the world and destroy the goodness in people, thus the events of *The

Nun set up the clash twenty years in the future between Valak and the Warrens.

The Nun ultimately tells the story of how Valak emerged into the world, despite the best efforts of Sister Victoria. Apparently Valak is confined in a catacomb behind a door marked "*Finit hic Deo*" ("God ends here"). While it is not clear why Sister Jessica and Sister Victoria must enter this area, especially considering "the evil needs a vessel to escape," Jessica is killed and Victoria hangs herself rather than allow Valak to use her to break free. In 1952, the Vatican sends Sister Irene (who has not taken her final vows yet and is thus still a novice) and Father Burke to the Abbey of St. Carta in Romania to investigate the suicide. They discover a number of dead nuns, whom they bury. It is left ambiguous as to whether the nuns still at the convent are alive, ghosts or demonic (other than Valak).

A variety of illusions and spiritual attacks occur. Father Burke ends up buried. Frenchie is assaulted. Finally, they enter the catacombs and fight Valak. They have a secret weapon, however – a small vial of the actual blood of Christ. Stealing an ending from *Tales from the Crypt: Demon Knight* (1995, Ernest Dickerson), *The Nun* has Sister Irene place the blood in her mouth and spit it at Valak, who is then seemingly returned to hell; the audience is shown, however, that Valak was also able to possess Frenchie and therefore was able to leave the abbey and enter the world. As noted above, in an epilogue of sorts, the film returns to the lecture at Massachusetts Western University depicted in *The Conjuring* in which Frenchie, now going by his birth name, Maurice Theriault, was subsequently exorcized by the Warrens, further pushing Valak into the world and continuing the war between the demon and the couple.

As Eve Tushnet argues, *The Nun* presents a genuine theological theme, highlighting "the fear of losing one's faith and identity," even in the heart of a place of faith (2018). *The Nun*, Tushnet states, "is about fear of submission; fear of betrayal, of being abandoned and destroyed by God and the church who promised to save you; fear of giving yourself, body and soul, in the hope that this plunge into God will strengthen you instead of destroying you" (2018). Sister Irene (whose name means "peace") is a novitiate, not yet a full nun. The film implies a life of poverty, chastity and obedience might not be the best path for her. However, before the climactic battle, she asks Father Burke to guide her through her full vows, so she might face Valak as a complete nun. It is a leap of faith

– a decision to commit fully to God and hope that her surrender to the Lord will give her power to conquer demons. The film bears this hope out, matching the faith of the Warrens in *The Conjuring* and *The Conjuring 2*.

Despite this theological aspect, the movie remains problematic as both a stand-alone film and a prequel to *The Conjuring*.

THE CURSE OF LA LLORONA (2019)

The prologue begins in Mexico in 1673 in which a young mother drowns her two boys and then herself when she learns her husband has cheated on her. This is the origin of La Llorona, the "wailing woman" of Mexican mythology, a demonic spirit that stalks the earth looking for children to replace the ones she killed. It is a cautionary tale designed to encourage children to behave, but also links genetically to the other *Conjuring* films. La Llorona, like Bathsheba and Annabelle, is a female spirit driven to harm children. The film then jumps to 1973, the year *The Exorcist* was released, and Los Angeles. Anna, a widowed social worker with a daughter and a son, carries out a welfare check on Thomas and Carlos, the two sons of Patricia Alvarez. Anna finds the boys locked in a closet covered in writing and crucifixes and removes the children from the home. In doing so, she exposes the boys to La Llorona, who tracks down the children to a Catholic boys' home and takes them, drowning them in a river. Anna's intervention also attracts La Llorona's attention towards her own children.

As strange things begin to occur around the house, including visions of La Llorona and her attempt to drown Sam, Anna's daughter in the bathtub, Anna turns to Father Perez from *Annabelle* for help. He recommends she speak with Rafael, who used to be a priest, now a *curandero*, a traditional Latin American healer. Patricia also comes to Anna's house, swearing revenge and attempting to steal Anna's children to use them to bargain with La Llorona for her own. Rafael uses various rituals to force La Llorona to reveal herself, to block her from entering the home, and finally to banish her. Raymond Cruz plays him with a deadpan humor that does not erase the construction of him as some sort of shaman who uses a kind of witchcraft.

The film's politics have come under fire for "whitewashing" a Mexican story. Tyler Unsell also argues that the film reinforces stereotypes of Latinas, single mothers, and Latin culture (2019). Rafael's "magic" is used to battle a Latina monster and clearly divides America into the (white) world of helpful social workers, science, Christianity and affluence and the Latinx world of superstition, poverty, witchcraft and a need for social workers (Unsell 2019). The film itself also has been criticized as moving further and further away from what made *The Conjuring* an effective horror film. "It relies heavily on jump scares rather than anything existentially terrifying, and there are leaps in narrative logic that don't quite make sense," states Katie Walsh in the *Los Angeles Times* (2019, E8). She also finds the script "lightweight" (2019, E8). It has its moments and echoes *The Conjuring* in the idea of a supernatural, dead mother that seeks the death of children. Sadly, La Llorona herself, however, is no Bathsheba Sherman.

ANNABELLE COMES HOME (2019)

Released only two months after *The Curse of La Llorona*, and written and directed by Gary Dauberman, the screenwriter of *Annabelle*, *Annabelle: Creation*, and *The Nun*, *Annabelle Comes Home* is an example of the law of diminishing returns. The *New York Times* review called it "a shameless franchise-stuffer" and "lethargic," and claims it "delivers an abundance of haunted-house clichés and few genuine scares" (Catsoulis 2019). The review is sadly correct. The film is predictable and even at times silly verging on campy (see: ghost werewolf defeated by hitting it with a guitar).

The title comes from a line in Bee's journal in *Annabelle: Creation*, further cementing the links between the films in the series. The diary was kept by young Annabelle "Bee" Mullins until her death in a car accident. In that film, young orphan Janice finds it in Bee's room and looks through it. After several blank pages following the last entry, in a child-like scrawl is written, "Dear Diary – today is the day I came home." The title is ironic in a sense: Annabelle did not ever actually come home – a demon used the doll as a conduit to terrify first the Mullins and their wards, then the Forms, and then some student nurses through the series. The entity that uses the doll seeks a "home" – a human body to possess and use. As noted at the start of this volume, ultimately, the *Conjuring* films are about possessions, not hauntings.

THE CONJURING

The film begins with the acquisition of Annabelle by the Warrens, who use former church materials to build a glass case to hold Annabelle after several paranormal experiences on the road home from the nurse's apartment. In this pre-credit sequence, the audience also learns Annabelle is not only a conduit for a demon, it is also "a beacon for other spirits." In other words, its very presence summons supernatural entities. Using glass from a dismantled church, they build Annabelle's box. "Is it safe?" asks Ed. "The evil is contained," reassures Lorraine. But those are not the same thing.

A year later and the couple's daughter, Judy Warren, faces challenges at school because of her parents' vocation and recent reports in the media that they are frauds. Credit is due to the film for depicting how the parents' work isolates the child. "I'm sorry I can't come to your birthday party," a sad friend tells Judy, "my parents say I'm not ready to process death." "It's a birthday party," says Judy, incredulous. The empty school hallway in which she finds herself is a literalization of her loneliness and isolation. Judy is also shown to share her mother's abilities, seeing spirits, including the ghost of a priest, as well as intuiting things about others. She knows, for example, that Daniela's father has died, though no one has told her.

The Warrens have a case, so Judy is left in the care of teen babysitter Mary Ellen, whose friend Daniela tags along, with an ulterior motive – since the death of her father in an accident she wants to contact him and assumes the Warren house will have the tools to do so. She inadvertently releases Annabelle and a number of other spirits, including a haunted wedding gown, a spirit called "the Ferryman" that appears as a corpse with coins over his eyes ("If you don't pay his toll, he'll take your soul" – an obvious reference to Charon, the Greek mythological boatman of the dead, taking the nominally Christian worldview of the *Conjuring* Universe and adding Greek myth), and the ghost of a werewolf. The entire second act of the film involves the three young woman and neighbor Bob, a young man, running around the Warren household, attempting to escape spirits. The Warrens return and resolve everything, putting the genies back in their bottles.

With its young protagonists and *Goosebumps*-meets-*Adventures-in-Babysitting* vibe, the film was referred to in a *Forbes* review as "*Conjuring Jr*" aimed at "the sleepover crowd," which seems appropriate (Mendelson 2019). Yet even the *Forbes* review, as well as reviews in *Rolling Stone* and the *Los Angeles Times* were positive overall, and found the film to be a different and fun addition to *The Conjuring* universe (Fear 2019; Walsh 2019b). We might note that "fun" was never a word attached to the original film. Scary, yes, well-made, yes, but not a "fun" film. *Annabelle Comes Home* is fun but lacks the essential elements that made *The Conjuring* into such a successful horror film.

More films are in the works for *The Conjuring* universe. That might not continue the legacy of the first. As Katie Walsh observes in her review of *The Curse of La Llorona* for the *Los Angeles Times*:

> The "Conjuring" spinoffs are like photocopies – each new iteration comes out to diminished returns. The structure, ideas and style are there, but there isn't the same heft of themes or slick craft Wan expressed in his two "Conjuring" films. (2019, E8)

This observation is a fair criticism (there is a reason, after all, that the main subject of this volume is *The Conjuring* and not *The Curse of La Llorona* or *The Nun*). The lack of consistent quality and horror in the films of the *Conjuring* Universe seems to suggest this volume's initial contention: that it is James Wan who, with his "magician's assistants," crafts films that terrify through careful, calculated effect, while still presenting serious themes and ideas. Wan has remained a presence as the producer or executive producer of all the *Conjuring* films (and is also credited for co-writing the story of *Annabelle Comes Home*), but it is his skills as a director, not a producer, that makes *The Conjuring* so effective.

There is now the promise of at least three more films in *The Conjuring* Universe. As of this writing, *The Conjuring 3*, produced by Wan and directed by Michael Chaves, was released in June 2021, having been postponed from 2020 due to the COVID-19 pandemic. *The Conjuring 3* concerns the case of Arne Cheyenne Johnson and the Glatzel family, also known as "The Devil Made Me Do It" case, in which Johnson killed his landlord after being possessed by a demon that the Warrens had exorcized from 11-year-old David Glatzel. Johnson's attorney argued "not guilty" by reason of demonic possession, which the trial judge rejected (see Brittle 1983). The film, directed by *The Curse of La Llorona*'s Michael Chaves, contains many of the elements of the first two, but serves more as a tribute to the power of the original in that it fails to replicate the terror of the original *Conjuring*. It also drifts even further away from the source story, introducing a conspiracy of Connecticut witches and a priest with a demonic illegitimate daughter behind the horrors. While containing all the aspects that made the original memorable and terrifying, the film ultimately fails to tie them together. *The Nun 2* is also in development at Atomic Monster, as is *The Crooked Man*, a story based around the apparition in *The Conjuring 2* that, like the nun, is seemingly a manifestation of Valak.

In conclusion, the *Conjuring* Universe consists of not just sequels and prequels, but is a series of intertextual narratives. Perhaps it is more useful to think of the films not as a universe, but as the many branches of *The Conjuring* tree. Each branch remains its own, but together they also form a single unified thing – smaller than a universe perhaps, but large enough to dwarf individuals and provide a huge, expansive narrative. Some branches are stronger than others, some branches are more developed than others, but all remain part of the same thing, grown from a single seed.

Conclusion: What Exactly is Conjured in *The Conjuring*?

We close with an exploration of the title itself and a brief consideration of the larger context. If, as the *OED* suggests, the meaning of a conjuring is "to cause (a spirit or ghost) to appear by means of a magic ritual," then the title is a lie. Bathsheba Sherman is not conjured in the film – she is already present in the house. Nothing is conjured into the doll Annabelle – whatever lurks inside the doll is already present when the doll was given to the young nurses. There are no magic rituals except an exorcism (designed to make Bathsheba disappear), and the spirit is already there when the family moves in. Therefore, I suggest that the title refers to the film itself and not what occurs in it. *The Conjuring* is a ritualistic retelling of the Perron family haunting designed to cause a spirit of terror in the audience. Wan, as I have suggested several times in the book, is the conjurer, the magician telling us to look over there and then performing the trick, over and over again, terrifying the audience with what he summons. *The Conjuring* is also a series of magic tricks within a magic trick

"Conjurer" also carries negative connotations – a trickster performing sleight of hand, but nothing more. The famous French magician Jean Eugène Robert-Houdin (himself called "King of the Conjurors") states, "A conjuror…is an actor playing the part of a magician" (1878, 43). In other words, for Robert-Houdin, a stage magician and entertainer, a conjuror was nothing more or less than any other performer – someone who crafts polite fictions for entertainment purposes. Conversely, within his own life the magician John Dee was considered a conjuror, as written by a contemporary in 1577: "Dee was not just a conjuror of devils but 'The Great Conjuror: and so, (as some would say), the *Arch-Conjuror* of this whole kingdom'" (quoted in Parry 2013, 67, emphasis in original). Dee was known for his ability to conjure spirits and was an advisor to Queen Elizabeth. Although some considered him to be a conjuror of the sort Robert-Houdin describes, many others felt he could actually traffic with spirits and magic. The term thus carries a tension between the occult and entertainment. The term might therefore be appropriate for the Warrens, who, as chapter two outlined, are regarded by some as having actual knowledge and powers to fight demons and evil spirits and by others as being entertainers, mountebanks and charlatans – frauds who knew how to put themselves at the center of every story.

"Conjure" is also often attached to magical women, particularly dangerous ones. Fritz Leiber's *Conjure Wife* (1943) narrates the tale of a small-town professor who learns his wife is a witch who has secretly used her powers to support and develop his career, further learning that conjuring and witchcraft is an open secret among women and completely unknown by men. It has inspired at least three films: *Weird Woman* (1944, Reginald LeBorg), *Burn, Witch, Burn!* (released in the UK as *Night of the Eagle*, 1962, Sidney Hayers), and *Witches' Brew* (1980, Richard Shorr, Herbert L. Strock), and shaped subsequent contemporary witch stories. Given the danger in the film comes from primarily female figures – Annabelle, Bathsheba – and that Lorraine is the "sensitive," whereas Ed is the demonologist (she the one who interacts with spirits, he the one that banishes them), the idea of a "conjure woman" is certainly present throughout the film. A "conjure woman" is a sorceress, particularly one that practices voodoo or hoodoo and the term is colloquial to the American south. African-American writer Charles W. Chesnutt entitled his 1899 seminal fiction collection *The Conjure Woman*, the frame of the volume being a white northerner who wants to share the "conjure tales" told to him by a freed black slave.

In chapter one, I referred to James Wan as the arch-conjuror of the film, the magician who entertains but also reveals something of a darker truth. While the "true story" of the marketing claims may be a bit of a stretch, the idea of *The Conjuring* as one of the scariest films of its decade is not. I find myself agreeing with Tomris Laffly, who observed that what is summoned in *The Conjuring* is "the underlying anxieties of the vulnerable everyman" (2016). Fear of economic instability drives Roger and Carolyn to purchase a house that may be haunted and for Roger to accept jobs that pay less than his usual rate and keep him away from his family longer. Fear for one's children drives all four parents in the film – concern that they might be harmed or die young. The film expresses a number of common fears: fear of invasion of one's own home; fear of being manipulated by forces beyond your control; fear that the past may not be past but will come back to cause harm; fear that things that one has nothing to do with will nevertheless profoundly affect one's life; and simple childhood fears returned in adulthood such as fear of the dark, fear of the cellar, fear of ghosties and witches and long-legged beasties. None of these childhood anxieties are rational, but that is the point. *The Conjuring* tells audiences their irrational fears *are* rational. There really is something lurking in the basement. That noise you heard from downstairs at night was something creepy. In fact, the gift of *The Conjuring* is that it actually reassures audiences. It tells them they are right to be afraid, they are right to be paranoid, and that institutions such as the Church and the government will not help the "little guy" when bad things happen. For that, we must turn to helpers such as the Warrens. The victims in *The Exorcist* are a famous movie star and her privileged daughter. The victims in *The Conjuring* are, by contrast, a working-class family. Chris MacNeil, who dines at the White House and has access to the best doctors and the Church hierarchy, acquires Lankaster Merrin, a world-famous Jesuit, as her exorcist. The Perrons get a working-class demonologist in Ed Warren. He can tell you what is haunting your house and then stick his head under the hood and tell you why your Chevy won't run. What is conjured in *The Conjuring* is a scenario in which a working-class family is subjected to violence, intimidation and terror by a supernatural entity, and working-class paranormal investigators resolve that situation. What is conjured is fear for the little guy and hope that the little guy not only can be saved but will be.

The Conjuring has also conjured other films created in its wake. After seeing *The Conjuring*, André Øvredal (*Trollhunter*, 2010) was inspired to make *The Autopsy of Jane Doe* (2016), for example. With the release of each new iteration of the *Conjuring* Universe, the shaping influence of the original in horror cinema can be seen not just in in other films set there, but in the imitations of *The Conjuring* which have followed. It seems also safe to say that Netflix has proven to be a boon to the film, as it was released as video stores were closing and streaming services were replacing them. *The Conjuring* did great box office in the theatre but has also found an afterlife in streaming and video forms. What is conjured in *The Conjuring* is a legacy of haunted house and possession films shot in the style of Wan – frequently imitated, rarely duplicated.

As I was finishing this book, Lorraine Warren passed away on 18 April 2019. She was buried next to Ed in an allegedly haunted cemetery in Monroe, Connecticut, which only seems appropriate (LeBlanc 2019). It also would seem to indicate that what is being conjured in *The Conjuring* is the legacy of the Warrens that they would have wanted. Despite the controversy, the salacious accusations, and the allegations of fraud, the memory of the Warrens in popular culture will now always and forever be shaped by

The Conjuring franchise. James Wan has not only made the Warrens respectable, he has made them heroic, romantic and laudable. The Warrens of *The Conjuring*, while not the actual Warrens, is how they would have seen themselves, and how they would have wanted to be remembered.

In summary, *The Conjuring* is an effective, good, old-fashioned horror film. It is genuinely scary and anxiety-inducing. It is greater than the sum of its parts and it is greater than its marketing campaign of "based on a true story" would seem to suggest. What is conjured in *The Conjuring* are the demons that Ed warned me and my friend Tom about that snowy afternoon years ago, and that every horror fan still wants to see.

Notes

1. The full story of Annabelle (as the Warrens tell it) can be found in Gerald Brittle, *The Demonologist* (New York: St. Martin's, 1980), 41-56.
2. See https://en.wikipedia.org/wiki/The_Conjuring_Universe, for example.
3. Guy Lyon Playfair, *This House Is Haunted* (New York: Stein and Day, 1980). Even the Wikipedia page for the Enfield poltergeist mentions Ed only in passing, as part of professional skeptic Joe Nickell's alleged debunking of the Enfield case (https://en.wikipedia.org/wiki/Enfield_Poltergeist).
4. At the beginning of their investigatory career, when Lorraine sensed a house was haunted, Ed would paint a canvas of the house. The Warrens would then knock on the door and offer the painting for free in exchange for permission to investigate the place. Ed's painting of the nun in *The Conjuring 2* is a direct reference to both Ed's background as a painter and his supernatural subject matter.

BIBLIOGRAPHY

Alexander, Bryan. (2013) "The 'true' story behind 'The Conjuring'" *USA Today* (July 22). http://usatoday.com/story/life/movies/2013/07/22/conjuring-true-story-perron/2457209

Andreeva, Nellie. (2013) "What's in A Title? 'The Conjuring' Producer and New Line In Dispute Over TV Rights" *Deadline.com* (June 21). https://deadline.com/2013/06/whats-in-a-title-the-conjuring-producer-new-line-head-to-arbitration-over-tv-rights-527167/

Bartholomew, Robert E. and Joe Nickell. (2015) *American Hauntings: The True Stories Behind American's Scariest Movies from The Exorcist to The Conjuring*. Santa Barbara: Praeger.

Bendici, Ray. (2009) "Damned Interview: Ray Garton." *Damned Connecticut* (March). http://www.damnedct.com/damned-interview-ray-garton

Berlatsky, Noah. (2013) "*The Conjuring*: A Dull Lesson in the Horrors of 'Based on a True Story'" The Atlantic (July 19). https://www.theatlantic.com/entertainment/archive/2013/07/-i-the-conjuring-i-a-dull-lesson-in-the-horrors-of-based-on-a-true-story/277938/>

Bibbliani, William. (2018) "'The Conjuring' Movies, Ranked Worst to Best" *The Wrap* (September 5): http://www.thewrap.com/the-conjuring-movies-ranked-worst-to-best/

breakingthefragile (2013). "Review: Joseph Bishara *The Conjuring*." Sputnik Music.com (July 25). https://www.sputnikmusic.com/review/58097/Joseph-Bishara-The-Conjuring/

Brittle, Gerald. (1980) *The Demonologist: The True Story of Ed and Lorraine Warren, The World-Famous Exorcism Team*. New York: St. Martin's.

Brittle, Gerald. (1983) *The Devil in Connecticut*. New York: Bantam.

Buckwalter, Ian. (2013) "Did *The Conjuring* Really Deserve an 'R' Rating Just for Being Scary?" *The Atlantic* (July 22). <https://www.theatlantic.com/entertainment/archive/2013/07/did-em-the-conjuring-em-really-deserve-an-r-rating-just-for-being-scary/277965/>

Burton, Chris, ed. (2017) *Traditional & Revised Catholic Rites of Exorcism* (English). Middletown, DE: Burton.

Campus Circle Staff. (2014) "Annabelle Isn't Child's Play…She's the Real Deal" *Campus Circle* (October 1-8): 14.

Catechism of the Catholic Church. (1994) New York: William H. Sadler.

Catsoulis, Jeannette. (2019) "'Annabelle Comes Home' Review: An Evil Doll Returns and She's Not Alone." *New York Times* (June 24): https://www.nytimes.com/2019/06/24/movies/annabelle-comes-home-review.html

Chang, Justin. (2013) "'Conjuring' Up a Winner." *Variety* 320 (July): 88.

Collins, Brian. "The Conjuring," *Religious Studies Review* 39.4 (December 2013): 253-4.

Collis, Clark. (2013) "Director James Wan talks 'The Conjuring' and 'Insidious 2' and confirms we'll be seeing more of [spoiler] in 'Fast & Furious 7'" *Entertainment Weekly* (June 20). https://ew.com/article/2013/06/20/fast-and-furious-7-conjuring-insidious-2-james-wan/

Cowan, Douglas E. (2008) *Sacred Terror: Religion and Horror on the Sacred Screen.* Waco, TX: Baylor University Press.

Dargis, Manohla. (2013) "Homeownership Has Its Perils." *New York Times* (July 18). https://www.nytimes.com/2013/07/19/movies/the-conjuring-puts-lili-taylor-in-a-haunted-house.htm

Dean, Tres. (2019) "The Scariest Part: A Round of Applause for 'The Conjuring'" *Geek.com.* (October 10). https://www.geek.com/movies/the-scariest-part-a-round-of-applause-for-the-conjuring-1807003/

Dowd, A.A. (2013) "Movie Reviews: The Conjuring" *A.V. Club* (July 18). https://film.avclub.com/the-conjuring-1798177413.

Durlade, Alonso. (2013) "'The Conjuring' Review: No, Seriously, Do NOT Go in the Basement" *The Wrap* (June 22). https://www.thewrap.com/conjuring-review-no-seriously-do-not-go-basement-99116/

Eaton, Marc A. (2015) "'Give Us a Sign of Your Presence:' Paranormal Investigation as a Spiritual Practice." *Sociology of Religion.* 76.4: 389-412.

Eaton, Marc A. (2019) "Manifesting Spirits: Paranormal Investigation and the Narrative Development of a Haunting." *Journal of Contemporary Ethnography* 48.2: 155-182.

Eckstrom, Kevin. (2013) "Can a horror film lead to God?" *National Catholic Reporter* (August 16-29): 18.

Fear, David. (2019) "'Annabelle Comes Home' Review: Hello, Evil-Hellspawn Dolly!" *Rolling Stone* (June 2). https://www.rollingstone.com/movies/movie-reviews/annabelle-comes-home-movie-review-851030.

Fichera, J. Blake. (2016) *Scored to Death: Conversations with Some of Horror's Greatest Composers*. Los Angeles: Silman-James Press.

Hale, Mike. (2009) "Consigning Reality to Ghosts." *New York Times* (December 10).

Hesse, Josiah H. (2016) "Why Are So Many Horror Films Christian Propaganda?" *Vice.com* (October 19). http://www.vice.com/read/why-are-so-many-horror-films-christian-propaganda.

Hill, Sharon A. (2017) *Scientifical Americans: The Culture of Amateur Paranormal Researchers*. Jefferson, N.C.: McFarland.

Howe, Katherine, ed. (2014) *The Penguin Book of Witches*. New York: Penguin Books.

John XXIII. (1962) *Gaudet Mater Ecclesia*. http://w2.vatican.va/content/john-xxiii/la/speeches/1962/documents/hf_j-xxiii_spe_19621011_opening-council.html.

King, Stephen. (1981) *Danse Macabre*. New York: Berkeley.

Kristeva, Julia. (1982) *The Powers of Horror: An Essay on Abjection*. New York: Columbia University Press.

Laffly, Tomris. (2016) "The Conjuring 2" *Film Journal International* vol. 119: issue 7.

LeBlanc, Jocelyne. (2019) "Lorraine Warren Will Be Buried in Haunted Cemetery." *Mysterious Universe* (April 24). https://mysteriousuniverse.org/2019/04/lorraine-warren-will-be-buried-in-haunted-cemetery/

Leiber, Fritz. (1991) *Conjure Wife*. (1943) New York: Tor.

Lennard, Dominic. (2014) *Bad Seeds and Holy Terrors: The Child Villains of Horror Film*. Albany: State University of New York Press.

Lovecraft, Howard Phillips. (1973) *Supernatural Horror in Literature*. New York: Dover.

Martin, Malachi. (1977) *Hostage to the Devil*. New York: Bantam.

Masters, Kim and Ashley Cullins. (2017) "War Over 'The Conjuring': The Disturbing Claims Behind a Billion-Dollar Franchise." *The Hollywood Reporter* (December 13). https://www.hollywoodreporter.com/features/war-conjuring-disturbing-claims-behind-a-billion-dollar-franchise-1064364.

Mather, Cotton. (1971) *Selected Letters*. Edited by Kenneth Silverman. Baton Rouge, LA: Louisiana State University Press.

Mather, Cotton. (1862) *The Wonders of the Invisible World: The Trials of the Witches*. (1693) Amherst, WI: Amherst Press.

Mendelson, Scott. (2019) "'Annabelle Comes Home' Review: It's 'Goosebumps' Story Within the 'Conjuring' Universe." *Forbes* (June 26). https://www.forbes.com/sites/scottmendelson/2019/06/26/review-box-office-annabelle-comes-home-conjuring-mckenna-grace-patrick-wilson-vera-farmiga-katie-sarife-madison-iseman-gary-dauberman/#3f335b230a72

Motion Picture Association of America, (2010) "Classification and Rating Rules," https://www.filmratings.com/Content/Downloads/rating_rules.pdf (January 1), 8.

Murphy, Bernice M. (2015) "'It's Not the House That's Haunted': Demons, Debt, and the Family in Peril in Recent Horror Cinema" in *Cinematic Ghosts*, ed. Murray Leeder. London: Bloomsbury.

"New Line Cinema's 'Conjuring' Universe Surpass $1 Billion at the Global Box Office." (2019). *Plus Company Updates* 21 August 2017. Business Insights: Global. Web. (February 25). http://bi.galegroup.com/global/article/GALE/%7CA501254283

Nickell, Joe. (2014) "*The Conjuring*: Ghosts? Poltergeists? Demons?" Skeptical Inquirer 38.2: 22-25.

Nickell, Joe. (2016) "Dispelling Demons: Detective Work at The Conjuring House" Skeptical Inquirer 40.6: 20-24.

O'Hehir, Andrew. (2013) ""The Conjuring": Right-wing, woman-hating and really scary" Salon.com. (July 18). https://www.salon.com/2013/07/18/the_conjuring_right_wing_woman_hating_and_really_scary/

Otto, Rudolf. (1958) The Idea of the Holy. Oxford: Oxford University Press.

Outlaw, Kofi. (2013) "'The Conjuring' Review" Screenrant (July 19). https://screenrant.com/the-conjuring-reviews-2013/

Parry, Glynn. (2013) Arch-Conjurer of England: John Dee. New Haven: Yale University Press.

Perron, Andrea. (2011). House of Darkness House of Light Volume One. Bloomington, IN: AuthorHouse.

---. (2013) House of Darkness House of Light Volume Two. Bloomington, IN: AuthorHouse.

---. (2014) House of Darkness House of Light Volume Three. Bloomington, IN: AuthorHouse.

Peterson, Joseph H., ed. and trans. (2001) The Lesser Key of Solomon. York Beach, ME: Weiser Books.

Playfair, Guy Lyon. (1980) This House Is Haunted. New York: Stein and Day.

Poole, Benjamin. (2012) Devil's Advocates: Saw. Leighton Buzzard: Auteur.

Radford, Benjamin. (2009) "The Real Story Behind 'The Haunting in Connecticut'" Live Science (March 26). https://www.livescience.com/5346-real-story-haunting-connecticut.html

Ratzinger, Joseph Cardinal. (1985) "Letter to Ordinaries regarding norms on Exorcism," (September 28). http://www.vatican.va/roman_curia/congregations/cfaith/documents/rc_con_cfaith_doc_19850924_exorcism_en.html

Robert-Houdin, Jean Eugène. (1878) The Secrets of Conjuring and Magic; or, How to Become a Wizard. Trans. and ed. Professor Hoffman. London: George Routledge and Sons.

Roberts, Robin. *Subversive Spirits: The Female Ghost in British and American Popular Culture.* Jackson: University Press of Mississippi, 2018.

Ryan, Jonathan. (2013) "Our Faith Led Us to Write a Horror Story." *Patheos* (July 12). http://www.patheos.com/blogs/geekgoesrogue/2013/07/our-faith-led-us-to-write-a-horror-story/

Schiff, Stacy. (2015) *The Witches: Salem, 1692.* New York: Little, Brown and Company.

Snellings, April. (2013) "Living with the Dead." *Rue Morgue* 135 (July): 30-32.

Subissati, Andrea. (2017) "Bonfires & Broomsticks: A Century of Witches," *Rue Morgue* 178 (Sept./Oct): 20.

Tushnet, Eve. (2018) "Review: 'The Nun' highlights the fear of losing one's faith and identity." *America* (September 13). https://www.americamagazine.org/arts-culture/2018/09/13/review-nun-highlights-fear-losing-ones-faith-and-identity

Unsell, Tyler. (2019) "In the Age of Trump, 'The Curse of La Llorona' is Not Helpful." *Signal Horizon* (April 25). https://www.signalhorizon.com/single-post/2019/04/24/In-the-Age-of-Trump-The-Curse-of-La-Llorona-is-not-helpful

Vancheri, Barbara. (2013) "Vera Farmiga didn't let fear interfere with 'The Conjuring'" *Pittsburgh Post Gazette* (July 19). https://www.post-gazette.com/ae/movies/2013/07/19/Vera-Farmiga-didn-t-let-fear-interfere-with-The-Conjuring/stories/201307190164

Voltaire. (1972) *Philosophical Dictionary*, trans. Theodore Besterman. New York: Penguin Books.

Walsh, Katie. (2019a) "'La Llorona' turns horror into schlock" *Los Angeles Times* (April 14): E8.

Walsh, Katie. (2019b) "'Annabelle' is apex of horror trilogy." *Los Angeles Times* (June 26): E2.

Warren, Ed, Lorraine Warren and Robert David Chase. (1989) *Ghost Hunters.* New York: St. Martin's.

Warren, Ed, Lorraine Warren, Carmen Snedeker, Al Snedeker and Ray Garton. (1992) *In a Dark Place: The Story of a True Haunting.* New York: Dell.

Weintraub, Steve. (2013) "Director James Wan Talks THE CONJURING, Deleted Scenes, Test Screenings, FAST AND FURIOUS 7, and INSIDIOUS 2" *Collider.com* (July 18). https://collider.com/james-wan-the-conjuring-fast-and-furious-7/.

Wetmore, Jr., Kevin J. (2012) *Post-9/11 Horror in American Cinema*. New York: Continuum.

DEVIL'S ADVOCATES

"Auteur Publishing's new Devil's Advocates critiques on individual titles offer bracingly fresh perspectives from passionate writers. The series will perfectly complement the BFI archive volumes." Christopher Fowler, Independent on Sunday

IT FOLLOWS – JOSHUA GRIMM

Amid a recent resurgence in horror films, David Robert Mitchell's It Follows *stands out as a particularly bold entry, a horror fan's dream come true that sparked a renewed creativity. Joshua Grimm focuses on how this film helped reinvent the rules of a horror movie, particularly along the lines of genre, style, sex, and gender.*

DAUGHTERS OF DARKNESS – KAT ELLINGER

A vampire film like no other, Daughters of Darkness *(1971) is a classic of high-Gothic cinema, loved for its art-house and erotic flavours. Kat Ellinger examines the film in the context of its contemporaries and argues for its place as an important evolutionary link in the chain of female vampire cinema.*

THE WITCH – BRANDON GRAFIUS

The first stand-alone critical study of The Witch *provides the historical and religious background necessary for a fuller appreciation, including an insight into the Puritan movement in New England, as well as situating the film within a number of horror sub-genres (such as folk horror) as well as its other literary and folkloric influences.*

www.ingramcontent.com/pod-product-compliance
Lightning Source LLC
Chambersburg PA
CBHW071413300426
44114CB00016B/2289